NEPAL
DEMOCRACY AT CROSS ROADS
(Post-1990 Dynamics, Issues and Challenges)

Nepal
Democracy at Cross Roads

(Post-1990 Dynamics, Issues and Challenges)

B.C. UPRETI

KANISHKA PUBLISHERS, DISTRIBUTORS
NEW DELHI-110 002

KANISHKA PUBLISHERS, DISTRIBUTORS
4697/5-21 A, Ansari Road, Daryaganj
New Delhi-110 002
Phones : 2327 0497, 2328 8285
Fax : 011-2328 8285
e-mail: kanishka_publishing@yahoo.co.in

First Published 2007

ISBN 81-7391-930-5

PRINTED IN INDIA

Published by Madan Sachdeva for Kanishka Publishers, Distributors, 4697/5-21A, Ansari Road, Daryaganj, New Delhi-110 002, Typeset by Sunshine Graphics, Delhi, and Printed at Nice Printing Press, Delhi.

Preface

Democracy is the most widely practiced form of governance in today's world system. As a concept it has been most durable in political science. Yet the history of democracy has been quite puzzling. It has indeed become a complex phenomenon. It is not easy to answer as to what is the nature and scope of democracy? However, what is good about democracy is that all kinds of state systems, all types of rulers aspire for being designated as a democratic state or a democratic ruler.

Nepal has a chequered history of democracy. The early phase of parliamentary democracy failed in Nepal with the royal take over in 1960. Nepal envisaged a third world model of democracy that actually provided a cover to the authoritarian rule of the monarchy. But this again failed and the democracy again stepped in through a national movement in 1990. The democratic process in the post 1990 period remained fragile; full of instability and uncertainty only to be replaced by the direct rule of the monarchy in 2005. Fortunately, it has proved to be a short lived experiment. The democratic forces are trying to comeback may be in a more determined way this time.

What is interesting in the case of Nepal is that while the authoritarian tendencies represented by monarchy have prevailed, the democratic forces have also been alive in the country. How long the people of Nepal will witness the struggle between monarchy and democracy is a serious issue.

Why has democracy failed in Nepal? Why has democracy succeeded in Nepal? What is the future of democracy in the country? Whether the people of Nepal have won the final struggle for democracy? These are important issues in the context of Nepal today.

This book is a modest attempt to understand these issues. There cannot be any definite and final answer to these and many other related issues. My effort has been to understand the pitfalls and the prognosis of democracy in a given situation. I have tried to take up a comprehensive view of democracy, with the understanding that the success or failure of democracy depends in the context of a given situation, where its operationalization takes place. What are the supportive structures? What are the destructive structures and who over powers whom? This is important in understanding course of democracy in a country.

In the pursuance of this study I have been benefited by a large number of persons. I woe a lot to my teachers, my Nepali and Indian friends with whom I had opportunity to discuss the issues which have been taken up here. I am grateful to my colleagues in the South Asia Studies Center for their encouragement and comments. I am thankful to Dr. S. N. Kaushik, Dr. Krishan Gopal, Dr. Surendra Chauhan and Dr. Shashi Upadhyaya.

The staff members of South Asia Studies Center Library deserve special thanks for their help in procuring the reading material.

I am extremely grateful to my family members: my brothers, sister-in-laws and others who have always encouraged me to work hard. My special thanks are to Ms Savita Upreti my wife and Neha and Navendu my daughter and son for their support and encouragement.

I would also like to extend my thanks to Itty Chacko and Mahendra Singh for taking up the burden in computerizing the Ms.

I would also like to extend my thanks to Shri Madan Sachdeva of Kanishka Publications for taking interest in the publication of this book.

There might have been shortcomings and gaps in the study for which I alone am is responsible.

Jaipur **B. C. Upreti**

Dated: 1 Dec., 2006

Contents

1

Democracy: Some Conceptual Issues

Democracy is a contemporary and most popular system of governance all over the world. Due to its wide spread popularity it has indeed become a compulsion. It is for this reason that irrespective of the nature and source of authority every country tends to present itself as a democratic political system. However, despite its popularity and universality, democracy as a concept has been quite controversial and complex. There have been too many definitions of democracy and many of them are just opposed to each other. In fact, what is democracy and how to define democracy has been a matter of one's own vested interest. Thus, a dictator can say that his country has democracy just by way of holding controlled elections. A super power may declare an authoritarian regime as democratic because it serves its vested interest. There are many examples in the history where a particular type of political experiment was levelled as a democracy by the rulers and tried to bring into forth a debate of western vis-a-vis indigenous models of democracy. Therefore, how to define democracy is a complex issue.

Another problem with the theoretical notions of democracy is related to the scope of democracy. Whether democracy is a system of governance or a way of life, whether it indicates at certain political institutions or the norms and values of a society as a whole? These are important issues in understanding the phenomenon of democracy.

The complications relating to the theoretical notions of democracy have arrived due to the fact that the countries of the third world represent a wide range of experiments with democracy. These varieties of democracy have also added to the theoretical complexities of democracy.

One would also like to add here that democracy is not a static phenomenon. The theoretical postulates of democracy have also changed in accordance to the changing nature of politics and society. It is, therefore, necessary to look into the conceptual framework of democracy in terms of its continuity.

In its initial phase democracy was viewed as an ideal conception. The people became the focal point of democratic governance and it was tried to bring forth that democracy was entirely related to people, nothing more and nothing less than that. Abraham Lincoln tried to focus upon the most idealist form of democracy when he stated that 'democracy is for the people, of the people and by the people.' Thus democracy was viewed as people's governance. But in practice it was found that democracy lacked all the three characteristics. It was neither people's governance nor it always worked for the interest of the people. A large number of scholars have defined democracy as a system in which people exercise powers through their representatives.[1] The people's participation in the exercise of powers vested on them was ensured during general elections. It was observed in many cases that even the popular participation could not be ensured.

The breakdown of democracy in many countries raised the question whether democracy meant political democracy alone or it required a broader perspective? Thus, the need to understand the different waves of democracies in the third world necessitated different theoretical postulates of democracy. However, it is interesting to note that there is no agreed perspective on democracy.

A Debate on the Concept of Democracy

Though a durable and popular idea in political science as mentioned earlier, democracy has been rather a complex idea and there have been complicating ideas about it.[2] There are varieties of scholars like Utilitarian, Liberals, to Social Democrats to Marxists, who have defined democracy differently.[3] Democracy is in fact, a dynamic concept and we agree with Arblaster when he states that:

> "There are three good reasons to think that those who try to define democracy only in terms of present days realities as a type of political system or culture which some societies

possess and others do not will find themselves left behind by history. Democracy is likely to remain not only a contestable concept: that is, a norm or ideal by which reality is tested and found waiting. There will always be some further extension or growth of democracy to be undertaken."[4]

There is a debate whether all people should be involved in governance in a democracy or only the representatives of the people or those rulers should be chosen by the ruled.[5] Schumpeter states that democracy does not and cannot mean that the people actually rule. They have the opportunity to accept or reject the persons who rule.[6] Scholars such as J.S. Mill, Larry Diamond, etc., have defined democracy in terms of political liberties and popular participation.[7] The representative democracy, the most popular form of democracy has been practically converted into a majoritarian democracy and as a result is has been a source of tensions in the multi-structured societies.

The issue whether democracy should be viewed as a form of government alone or it should also incorporate social and economic dimensions is also important.[8] In modern times democracy is being viewed as a comprehensive concept.

There are a number of contemporary writings on democracy that have taken a multiculturist view into account. They have criticized the majoritarian concept of democracy and have supported democracy as an instrument to accept existence of diverse groups and treat them on an equitable basis. John Dewey has viewed democracy in terms of freedom of cooperative individualities.[9] Rorty defines a democratic system in terms of existence of several national communities where political power does not remain confined to a dominant group.[10] Lyotard provides a strong criticism of the majoritarian democracy. He suggests that democracy is a system, which recognizes presence of various communities and ensures their participation in the political structures as multi-identities.[11]

It can be said that democracy has to develop itself as a measure of social, economic and political equalities ultimately. It is equally important that democracy is an adaptive and evolutionary process integrally linked to the process of social transformation.[12] It is also important to bear in mind that the process of democratization of polity must take in to account the political traditions and socio-cultural fabrics of the society. One significant issue related to democracy is its sustainability. How to ensure durability of democracy is an important question. In this regard, it has been opined by many scholars that whether democracy is imposed from above or from outside, its survival ultimately would depend on its ability to build deep-rooted cultural attachments among its people.[13] In fact, if we look into the third world context we find that democracy has received setbacks in many countries. There has been erosion of democracy or breakdown of democracy in many countries.[14] So the basic issue is that it is not sufficient to create democratic structures. It is equally important how people view about it, think about it and feel about it. The subjective well-being of people and interpersonal trust are important factors.[15] Thus, the cultural factor plays a crucial role in the sustenance of democracy.[16] Here again, the question of existence of cultures and their equitable preservation is an important issue in the stabilization and success of democracy.[17]

Political Leadership and Democracy

The role of political leadership is highly important in democracy. In fact, the success and failure of democracy rests much on the political leadership and political elite of the country. To what extent political leaders are committed to democracy is important. It is necessary that the democratic commitment of the political leadership is sustained with the change of political leadership. If this commitment is not transmitted to the coming generations of political leaders then it may result in the breakdown of democracy. It is, therefore necessary that the leadership should have a broader perspective and far sight ness.

Democracy needs consolidation and sustenance. It also depends to what extent the political leadership can incorporate different political forces and interests within the fold of the democratic system. In a democratic system consensus is essential. It is possible when the political leadership is not preoccupied with the vested political interests and develop pattern of collective interaction among different political leaders, groups and parties. Some studies indicate that the decay of democratic institutions in the third world countries is largely attributed to the self-serving actions and orientation of the political leadership. Thus, the role of leadership is important in democratic consolidation and sustenance.

Multiculturalism and Democracy

Multiculturalism and democracy are closely interlinked. It is only within the framework of a democratic polity that multiculturalism may flourish. It has been pointed out earlier that it is not sufficient that diverse cultural groups exist and interact with each other in a society. It is more important that they are treated equally. The issue of Multiculturalism is related to the fact that the cultural groups and communities occupying the same social sphere have the same status in public domain.[18] Thus multiculturalism speaks of equality of cultures. Democracy ensures that the socio-cultural identities based on caste, ethnicity, language, religion, race or gender does not become a source of discrimination and marginalization in the arena of public domain. Multiculturalism does not trust the process of establishing hegemony of majority community within the polity. It pleads for policies that protect diversity of cultures by enabling minority cultures operate on an equitable basis. Thus, it is more than a theory of minority rights as it supports the concept of democracy, where diverse cultural groups seek representation on an equitable basis.[19] In this way it can be argued that multiculturalism enrich the discourse of democracy in plural societies. Multiculturalism may be viewed as an important social and political agenda in this regard.[20]

State, Society and Democracy

The success of democracy rests to a large extent on the state–society relationship. There has to be a balance between the two. If there is no proper balance between the two and the state plays a role against the civil society, democracy cannot be sustained for a long time. In fact, it can be said that a liberal state and civil society are assets to democracy. There are a large number of examples in the third world where the authoritarian nature of the state did not allow democracy to function. If the state is authoritarian and centralized power will be exercised in a dictatorial manner. On the other hand, if a state is week, it will not be able to meet the expectations of the masses. In both the cases people will suffer and the civil society will came into confrontation with the state. The state-civil society conflict can prove to be a cause for the breaking of democracy.

There are many examples where the superiority of the state over civil society has lead to the erosion of the democratic political order.

It has also to be understood here that if the civil society is not in a position to assert its control over the supremacy of the state than the non-political institutions may become powerful in the exercise of the state authority. In many countries bureaucracy becomes a stakeholder in the political affairs of the state. While there are several other countries where militarisation of the state power takes place. Both the bureaucratic and militarized states have been a source of erosion of democracy in such countries. Therefore, a proper balance between state and the civil society is necessary for the endurance of democracy.

Political Parties and Democracy

Political parties are the instruments through which a democratic system is made functional. The political parties make a democracy operational. Hence, the sustainability of democracy depends on the nature of the political parties in a country. A strong party system is an asset to democracy.[21] On the contrary, weak and fragmented political parties are a curse over democracy.[22] The experience shows that there are very meager chances of the emergence of a majority and dominant party in the elections if political parties are fragmented and weak. This would naturally result in the formation of a weak coalition government. A weak coalition cannot provide a strong and stable government. If the government is not strong it cannot deliver goods to the people. Democracy cannot be successful if it fails in delivering goods. Therefore, it can be said that a strong party system is the lifeline of a successful democracy.

A successful party system is characterized by strong and wide social base of political parties, strong and charismatic leadership, ideological commitment, internal liberalization and decentralization, strong organizational base and mutual cooperation and understanding between different political parties.

It is necessary that the political parties have a popular support base. In some of the countries of the third world, the authoritarian rulers launched their own political party in order to acquire legitimacy for their authoritarian rule. Such political parties cannot serve the cause of democracy. So it is also important how the political parties take roots and what are its objectives.

Development and Democracy

There is a strong inter-relationship between democracy and development. However, it is controversial as what level of development is required for the successful working of democracy. It is not worth here to enter into this controversy, as it is difficult to reach to any definite conclusion. In a simple way it can be said that there is a two-way co-relationship between democracy and development.

The establishment of a democratic system arouses a large number of expectations of the people. It is believed that the democratic system would fulfill popular needs, aspirations and expectations in a reasonable way. If these expectations are not met it may give rise to popular discontent and dissatisfaction that may ultimately prove to be detrimental to the success of democracy.

The down of democracy in a country also gives way to the social and political mobilization of various marginalized groups and regions. These marginalized sections and regions of the society demand for an equitable share. It is necessary for a democratic order to accommodate these groups. The negligence on the part of the government towards these groups may result in various types of movements or conflicts such as ethnic tensions and conflicts, regional movements, communal conflicts and so on. All these conflicts and movements pose a serious challenge to democracy. It may be pointed out here that all these issues and problems are development related and they can be resolved by taking into consideration their problems, needs and aspirations.

It is now widely accepted that political democracy alone is not sufficient. It also requires social and economic democracy. The social and economic democracy means social parity and equitable access to resources and opportunities. This would again require a certain level of development as an essential prerequisite for the successful working of political democracy.

It may also be pointed out that a democratic state is bound to come under severe strain due to the growing demands by both the privileged and the under privileged sections of the society. These demands have to be accommodated and the state has to be responsive to them. Thus in a democracy government can acquire legitimacy only through continuous process of socio-economic development.

There are also examples where the authoritarian rulers initiate the process of socio-economic modernization in order to seek popular support and legitimacy. But after a certain stage of socio-economic transformation the state began to receive pressure from the society for political reforms and democracy. Thus, there is a casual relationship between democracy and development.

DEMOCRACY IN SOUTH ASIA

Democracy has been rather a recent phenomenon in South Asia. After independence from the colonial powers almost all the South Asian countries began with the politico-constitutional structures for the operationalisation of democracy. However, their main problem has been institutionalization of democracy as a core value of social and political life in few and the sustenance of democratic structures in others. The military coup in Pakistan in 1998 shows that the ground realities in some of these countries are quite different from what is actually required for the working of a democratic system. The different countries of the South Asian region have different experiences of democracy, ranging between western models of democracy to indigenous experiment though both failed in some.

Historico–Ideological Roots of Democracy

The concept of democracy developed in the West in a historical and evolutionary process. The rise of liberalism, nationalism, individualism and industrial capitalism contributed to the growth of democracy. Thus the idea of democracy grew in the society and developed in a gradual process. In contrast to this the emergence of democracy in the Indian sub-continent can be associated with the rise of national movement. It indeed became a corollary to anti-imperialism. The establishment of democratic institutions was considered to be the best model for the transfer of powers from the colonial rulers to the indigenous power elite. The democracy indeed became a corollary to anti-imperialism. The establishment of democratic institutions was considered to be the best model for the transformation of the colonial rule. The democracy indeed became a major aspect of nationalism that took roots during the era of nationalist movement. The political leadership and political parties who became the instrument of democracy sought their political training in the context of the British liberal democracy. Thus, the idea of democracy in South Asia was rooted in the history of national movement or in the idea of struggle against the authoritarian rule such as in Nepal.[23] The advocates of democracy believed that the idea of democracy would be realized as soon as the alien rule would come to an end.

Growth of Democracy

It was because of the impact of British liberal democracy that India, Sri Lanka, Pakistan, Nepal and later Bangladesh did not find it difficult initially, to establish democracy based on the British model of parliamentary form of government. It was considered to be a primary condition to promulgate a constitution based on the principles of popular sovereignty, rights and freedom. The constitution became the main vehicle of democracy and the primary agent of its implementation and protection. Thus, these countries envisaged the establishment of political democracy, which also suited to the interest of the political elite because it provided opportunity to them to become the power elite.

Since the establishment of a democratic government became a major instrument for the realization of the goals of national movement, the impulse of democracy remained strong so long as the thrust of national movement persisted. Also, it is for this reason that the democracy remained weak in the countries, which did not experience a national movement.

The democratic institutions took shape in South Asian countries in different ways. In India a broad based political structures were created within the framework of its constitution. India's secularism succeeded in encouraging a broad based political participation and despite various horizontal and vertical divisions within the society it could initiate a fairly successful democratic model. Provisions were made to bring various communities within the fold of the national political mainstream. But India could not build enough viable social and economic structures in order to accommodate various groups and regions within the political framework. Thus the notion of political democracy could not be equated with social and economic democracy. The secular trend also got weakened gradually. As a result Indian democracy faced numerous challenges.[24] It was in the context of these challenges that a debate was initiated to decide whether India needed a shift to the presidential system or should remain confined to the parliamentary democracy? More recently, a debate has again been started regarding the restructuring of the constitution. It is difficult to state whether the constitution of India has proved inadequate to face various challenges and has become incapable to resolve political problems or it is the power elite, which has made constitution a failure, therefore, problem does not relate to constitutional and political structures, but with the political processes and political actors? In any case such issues are bound to weaken the democratic favour in the country.

Pakistan also moved ahead with parliamentary democracy but the country could not sustain its democratic ethos and authoritarianism took its place. The army took over the powers and since then it has invariably ruled the country and controlled the democratic regimes when it was directly not in power. Pakistan has not been able to inculcate democratic values in the society due to authoritarianism and fundamentalism. Pakistan is still struggling with the problem of creating proper political and socio-economic structures for the working of a democracy. The non-political institutions are still overpowering politics for obvious reasons.

In Bangladesh also the rise of military in politics checked the growth of democracy. However, the country has succeeded in re-establishing democratic structures and processes after 1990. Although, Bangladesh still has a fragile democracy because of the fact that the offshoots of the erstwhile non–political power elite are significant in politics. Despite having a two party system Bangladesh has not been able to sustain democracy in terms of stability and growth in a strong way is an important issue.

In Sri Lanka parliamentary democracy came into operation soon after independence. But it failed in giving shape to a broad based nationalism. Instead, for its own survival, the power elite of Sri Lanka promoted cultural nationalism, which later on alienated the minority communities. The country had to move from one type of political set up to another. With the aggravation of ethnic conflict the country is faced with the problem of political instability and a threat to its national solidarity. Thus, it can be said that Sri Lanka had a majoritarian democracy wince the beginning promoting cultural ethos of the majority community, which alienated the minority groups.

In Nepal also a process of gradual democratization took place in 1951. But the democratic elite could not neutralize the political role of the traditional elite. As a result, the growth of democratic political institutions was slow and it paved a way for the re-emergency of monarchy to power in the name of so-called grassroot democracy. However, Nepal too has succeeded in re-establishing democracy in 1990.

It can be said on the basis of above brief discussion that democratic polity has survived in South Asia but most of the countries of South Asia have often lacked such political structures and institutions, which could sustain it on a long-term basis.

Like Indonesia, Egypt, Nigeria and Ghana, in South Asia also attempts were made to find out an alternative to the western liberal democracy. In Pakistan General Ayoob Khan established Basic Democracy in 1960 and in Nepal King Mahendra introduced Panchayat system in 1962. Their basic contention was that the western democracy based on party politics was not suitable to the conditions of the third world societies. Hence, such a model was needed which suited to their history and culture. The systems that these countries envisaged were stated to be the grassroot democracies. But in reality these were controlled democracies, aimed at providing a democratic cover to the authoritarian rule of the military general in Pakistan and the monarchy in Nepal. These systems allowed limited participation of people in the political process, hence proved to be inadequate in meeting popular demands and aspirations, and failed.

Good governance may be viewed as an indication of the successful working of democracy. Good governance is that which fulfill basic needs and aspirations of the people through maximum popular participation in the political affairs.

In the South Asian countries the constitutional system provides a basic framework for the operation of the governmental order. However, in practical terms two trends are visible in the context of all South Asian countries. Firstly, with regard to the working of the government there have been strong centralizing trends. The centralization of power has existed at all levels. These tendencies have resulted in the non-fulfillment of the needs and aspirations of the people on the one hand, and alienated various groups and communities from the governmental structures on the other. The centralizing tendencies within the governmental order have lead to the evolution of different models of government in different countries such as the priministerial system in India. Gaullist system in Sri Lanka, military–bureaucratic authoritarian state in Pakistan, patrimonial state in Nepal one man authoritarian rule in Maldives and so on. The centralization of political power has not only alienated the fringe support but has also given rise to protest movements of various magnitudes.

Two factors have been crucial in reducing centralization and discriminatory role of the state power. Firstly, the rise of middle class and its role in fighting against the authoritarian tendencies. Secondly, the rise in political consciousness among masses and broadening of the power structure through the use of ballot box. But there are problems with both. The middle class has been quite weak and fragmented in most of the South Asian countries and secondly, the general elections are becoming more ritualistic than the real test case for the past performance of a government.

Bureaucracy plays an important role in the success or failure of the governmental order in the South Asian countries. In Pakistan, Bangladesh and to some extent in Nepal politicization of bureaucracy has taken place and it has played an important role in the restructuring of governmental order. In India and Sri Lanka bureaucracy has received political patronage and acquired 'the steel frame' character. The bureaucracy has often been blamed for being suppressive in nature and serving the class interest and ignoring popular sentiments particularly where it is politicized and have a nexus with the political elite. Such trends have naturally been against the norms of democracy.

Concluding Observations

The forgoing discussion clearly indicates that democracy is a dynamic concept. Its meaning and nature has changed. Although there is no unanimity among scholars over the concept of democracy it can safely be said that democracy has to be viewed in a wider perspective. It is not a system of governance alone, rather it incorporates social values, norms and a way of life. Along with popular participation and rights it calls for social parity and equitable development. Democracy in its long-term perspective has to develop into a communitarian system, instead of a mere majoritarian rule.

Another important point is that the installation of democracy itself is not sufficient. It has to be sustained. The sustenance of democracy depends on a large number of factors such as the leadership role, parties, state–civil society relationship, levels of socio-economic development and soon. Therefore, the success and failure of democracy depends on the circumstances in which it operates.

The experiences of the third world countries regarding democracy are varied. Not only relating to the installation of democracy but also with regards to the endurance, breakdown, failure and the reinstallation of democracy. In fact, each of the countries of the third world provides a fascinating example of the success or breakdown of democracy.

REFERENCES

1. For a detailed study of the various explanations of democracy, see Robert A. Dahal, Democracy and its Critics, Cambridge Mass, 1989. *Larry Diamond, Developing Democracy Towards Consolidation,* Baltimore, John Hopkins University, 1999.
2. David Hold, *Models of Democracy*, Polity Press, Oxford, 1993: 2.
3. G. Sartori, *The Theory of Democracy Revisited,* Chattanm House Publishers, U.K., 1987.
4. Anthony, *Arblaster, Democracy*, World View Press, Delhi, 1997.
5. J. Levey, *Democracy, Basil Blackwell*, Oxford, 1978: 30.
6. J. Shumpeter, *Capitalism, Socialism and Democracy*, Allen and Unwin, London, 1876: 269.
7. See, John Stuart Mill, *On Liberty and Representative Government J.M. Dent,* London, 1976: 217; Larry Diamond, *et al.*, Democracy in Asia, Vistar Publishing House, New Delhi, 1989.
8. Larry Diamond, *et al.*, N. 7 : XVI.
9. John Dewey, *Freedom and Culture*, Popular Prakashan, 1966:113.
10. Richard Rorty, "Post-Modernist Bourgeois Liberalism" in Thomas Docherty (ed.), *Post-Modernism – A Reader,* Columbia University Press, New York, 1987: 23–225.
11. Jean Francois, Lyotard, *Quoted in Gurubhagat Singh,* "Post Modernist Difference in Democracy", in Gopal Singh (ed.), South Asia, New Delhi, 1998: 60.
12. D.L. Seth and Ashis Nandy (eds.), *The Multiverse of Democracy,* Sage Publications, New Delhi, 1996: 14.
13. Ronald Inglehart, "Trust Well Being and Democracy" in Mark E. Warren (ed.), *Democracy and Trust,* Cambridge University Press, 1999: 99.
14. See for some of the case studies in the Asian Context, Larry Diamond, *et al.,* (eds.), N. 7.
15. N. 13: 119.
16. See, Gabriel Almond and Sidley Verba, *The Civil Culture, Political*

Attitudes and Democracy in Five Nations, Princeton University Press, Princeton, 1963.

17. See for instance, Atul Kohli (ed.), *India's Democracy Princeton University Press, 1988;* N.G. Joyal, Democracy and the State Welfare, Secularism and Development in Contemporary India, Oxford University Press, New Delhi, 2001.
18. Gurpreet Mahajan, *The Multicultural Path: Issues of Diversity and Discrimination in Democracy,* Sage Publications, New Delhi, 2002.
19. N. 17.
20. Bill Martin, "Multiculturism : Consumerist or Transformational? "In Cynthia Willest (ed.), *Theorizing Multiculturism, A Guide to the Current Debate,* Blackwell, 1998.
21. There are many examples in India which indicate that the nature and style of democracy changed with the change of the party system and political parties.
22. See, Larry Diamond *et al.,* N. 7: 12-14 .
23. For some explanations and case studies, see Lok Raj Baral (ed.), *South Asia: Democracy and the Road Ahead,* POLSAN, Kathmandu, 1992.
24. See, Atul Kohli, *Democracy and Discontent, India's Growing Crisis of Governability,* Cambridge University Press, 1990; P. Dutt, Indian Democracy, New Challenges, Kanishka Publishers, New Delhi, 1996.

2

Installation and Breakdown of Democracy: The Backdrop

Among the countries of the South Asian region, Nepal provides a fascinating example of installation and breakdown of democracy. Despite the fact that Nepal was ruled by an authoritarian and autocratic ruler for a long time, it witnessed the down of democracy almost along with the countries that had witnessed a long drawn nationalist movement against the colonial powers, and where a gradual process of modernization and development along with modern politico-bureaucratic structures had begun. But it is a fact that after some initial headway democracy failed in the kingdom.

Nepal is among those countries of the third world that also tried to envisage an indigenous model of democracy. But this model could also not seek popular legitimacy and approval and it failed after a certain period of time.

Why democracy failed in Nepal is a major question today. Is it possible for the democratic elite of the country to learn from the history is an equally important issue. These two issues are important for an understanding of the complexities of democracy in Nepal in the post 1990 period.

It is with this objective in mind that we intend to briefly, look into the background and understand the evolution and growth of Nepali political system and its early struggle for democracy.

Evolution of Nepali State

Nepal is a small state situated along the southern slopes of the Himalayas. It separates the Gangetic plains of India in the south to the Tibetan plateau in the north. Despite being a small country it endows sharp geographical divisions ranging from steep snow clad mountains to middle hills and a small strip of plain area called Tarai towards the south, bordering the Indian region.[1] The geographical diversities along with landlocked nature of the country have affected distribution of resources, patterns of development as well as the patterns of power and authority.

The present day Nepal came into existence in 1769, after a process of annexation and secession of various principalities by King Prithvinarayan Shah of the Gorkha principality. A conspicuous feature of these principalities was the existence of perpetual rivalries among them.[2] The successors of King Prithvinarayan Shah continued with the policy of military adventurism in order to expand its boundaries further. After an initial success in Tibet they ultimately failed in northward expansion but succeeded in the south and extended its boundaries up to Kumoun and Garhwal in India. The international boundary of Nepal in the south was fixed in the treaty of Segauli in 1815. Afterwards Nepal never came in conflict with the British and maintained its independence, which gave the Nepalese a sense of superiority in comparison to the other South Asians.[3]

It is clear that the modern state of Nepal did not come into existence through a natural process but through a process of annexation and assimilation by the use of military force. It is true that the Nepali state did not get any challenge from any of its constituent afterwards and it remained an integrated whole. Nevertheless, it induced the characteristics of militarism, authoritarianism and despotism within the Nepali state.

The Shah rulers tried to lay a strong foundation of the monarchic rule on the basis of the Hindu philosophy of kingship. The king was incarnated as the representative of God (Lord Vishnu). He was the repository of all the powers and the religions sanctity that the institution of monarchy owned accorded him popular faith and support.

The monarchy laid down a strong social base for the support and sustenance of the kingship. A four-tier caste system was introduced and the roles of the various caste categories were decided on the basis of the hierarchy of the caste group. Thus, Brahmin and Kshatriya became the main pillars of the kingship. The various non-hindu tribal groups were brought under the fold of caste hierarchy through a process of Hinduaisation. It lead to the growth of a class which was socially on the top of the caste hierarchy, politically powerful and economically in possession of land and other privileges given by the monarchy. This privileged class along with the monarchy at the top became the main stakeholder in society, economy and polity. It naturally gave way to the emergence of a feudalistic order.

Shah and Rana Political Systems

The Shah rulers established a highly centralized political system in Nepal. The king held all civil and military powers. In order to laid down a strong foundation to the monarchic system King Prithvinarayan Shah relied heavily on the upper castes of the hills. The role and status of various caste categories was predetermined. The social hierarchy was important in seeking political and economic status. As a result, an in cohesive and pyramidal structure dominated by a handful of hill Brahmins and Kshatriyas characterized the Shah political system. Shifts and change in the power structure was confined to the elite families belonging to these castes. The principle of reward and punishment was also followed in appointments to administrative and military positions. The common man was treated as a subject and no rooms were left for political opposition and dissent.[4] The Shah rulers though tried to bring various ethnic groups within the fold of Hinduism. But still a large number of ethnic groups remained out of the fold of Hinduism. Thus, the society remained divided, horizontally as well as vertically. The Shah rulers created a myth of a monolithic society by the use of force. Nevertheless, the monarchic Shah political system and the priministerial Rana political system both were almost similar as far as the nature of the political system was concerned, except that both were run by different sets of political elite drawing from the same social strata.

The Shah rule came to an end in 1846 when Jung Bahadur established Rana political system after taking all powers from the monarch and declaring himself as the Prime Minister of Nepal. The Rana rulers also followed the centralized politico-administrative model of the Shah rulers, except that the members of the Rana family took place of various nobilities.[5] Jung Bahadur reinforced the caste hierarchies and modified various castes. Since the Rana's had come to power through a ghastly manner, they established a reign of tyranny in the country. No rooms were left for any kind of opposition. However, they could not prevent growth of opposition to their rule outside the country.[6] Those Nepalese who had come to India they started launching an origanised opposition to the Rana rule towards the 1930's. It acquired a concrete shape towards the end of the forties with the formation of Nepali Congress Party. Thus the Rana system faced popular opposition because of its highly authoritarian rule. It may be noted here that both the Shah and the Rana rulers tried to keep Nepal isolated from outside influences, underdeveloped and backward. But Rana's could not restrain a strong movement against it and the system collapsed in 1950, after a tripartite agreement concluded.

It may be pointed out here that both the Shah and the Ranas laid down a strong foundation of authoritarianism and centralization of power. It also laid down strong foundation of upper caste domination in politics and administration. The common men remained isolated from politico-administrative structures. The traditions of authoritarian power structure became so strong that the people did not have confidence about self-governance. The ruling elite had a closer alignment with the feudal class. Both the Shah and the Rana rulers tried to identify them with the state. Conspiracy was a major characteristic of Nepali politics. The power elite identified itself with the hill culture. Consequently identification with the hill culture became an essential pre-requisite for entering into politico-administrative structures. This alienated the people of Tarai.

Experiment in Democracy

The evolution of political process in Nepal has an enormous significance for the students of comparative politics and political modernization. In the course of a little more than two hundred years, the kingdom has experienced different forms of political transformations. The hereditary Shah rulers laid the foundation of a centralized authoritarian system that was followed by the Rana rulers who took over to power from the Shah Kings in 1846 and established their own despotic rule. It is interesting that the Ranas though established their own power the hereditary monarchy was maintained.

The process of democratization began in Nepal soon after the overthrow of the Rana political system in 1950. The movement against the Ranas took roots in the Indian soil, launched by those

Nepalese who were living in India and were highly inspired by the Indian National Movement. It was natural that they too were influenced by the western democratic ideology, particularly the parliamentary system. In 1951 when the coalition government consisting of the Nepali Congress and the Ranas came into existence it was expected to work for the establishment of democracy in the country. The parliamentary system, which was established in 1959 proved to be short-lived and was abrogated by King Mahendra in December 1960, to establish his own direct rule.[7] Before we proceed further it appears to be desirable to look into the issue that why democracy could not be sustained in the kingdom during the early period?

Actually two factors were important in bringing the 1950 revolution to an end. Firstly, the dramatic escape of King Tribhuwan from the royal palace to the Indian Embassy in Kathmandu, who was foreseeing restoration of his powers. Thus, before the movement could take roots in the kingdom it came to a sudden end. Secondly, in the New Delhi Agreement of 1951, India, because of the treaty that it had concluded with the Rana rulers, and also because of her own strategic interests in the Himalayan region, did not favour total uprooting of the traditional order. India's apprehensions were that a total uprooting of the traditional order might create political chaos, which would not be in her own interest. Nehru's middle way approach might be justified in the then prevailing conditions, but not from the point of view of the growth of democracy in the kingdom in the long run. The net result was that the 1950 movement was reduced to a mere restoration of powers of the monarchy. It did not help in the strengthening of democracy.

The Indian Memorandum of 8 December, 1950, as well as February 1951, New Delhi Agreement had emphasized the formation of a Constituent Assembly in order to prepare a new constitution for the Kingdom.[8] But this could never be materialized. Even in 1959 when the new constitution of Nepal came into force, king Mahendra did not accept demand for the formation of a Constituent Assembly and he himself promulgated the constitution. Thus a basic provision regarding the promulgation of the constitution through a duly elected Constituent Assembly could never be made effective in the Kingdom. This shows that the traditional elite was still assertive that it was not subscribed to democratic norms and beliefs; that it was interested in the democratization of the polity only to the extent which was essential in order to fulfill certain commitments on their part.

The political parties which played a major role in the over-throw of the Rana regime and which were expected to function for the stabilization of the democratic system failed to act in an appropriate direction. On the contrary, the manner in which the party politics went on, it only paved a way for the emergence of the Royal authority. It also gave an opportunity to the monarchy to label the activities of the political parties undemocratic and unfavourable to the prevailing conditions in Nepal. In fact, the Nepalese politics since 1951 was marked by the emergence of a large number of political parties and groups on the one hand and continuous fragmentation, group politics and personal rivalries among them on the other. Due to the endless rivalry and scramble for power among major political parties and politicians the goal of democracy was totally lost. The people were alienated. In fact, the political parties failed in providing leadership to the people. In their quest to acquire political power they had indeed, undermined the necessity of creating adequate socio-economic conditions for the sustenance of democracy in the Kingdom. It seems that the political parties lacked experience, and a sound mass base and a clear programme.

It paved a way for the re-emergence of traditional elite under the leadership of monarchy. The old land-owning classes and the Ranas found sufficient opportunities to further their sectional interests. They naturally got united to defeat reform measures of the Nepali Congress.[9] The people were hardly concerned about the emerging political patterns, since the basic socio-economic structure had remained unchanged, about which they were more concerned. The people lacked political consciousness as well. The army and bureaucracy also represented the bulk of the traditional interests of the society. It was very difficult to challenge their interests. The press which is considered to be a source of interest articulation and interest aggregation, remained largely devoid of this role. It may again be stressed here that the country lacked a feasible socio-economic infrastructural base for the working of democracy.

It should also be pointed out here that the nationalism, which took roots in Nepal towards the middle of the fifties was narrow based. In fact, the traditional elite in its quest for reassertion of political power, found India's special relationship with Nepal a major obstacle. Hence, it raised the boggy of anti-Indianism. It soon became a major tool of new Nepali nationalism. It was natural that the Nepalese ruling elite failed in developing a broad-based nationalism, which would have been supportive of democracy. Thus, the Nepali society lacked those basic premises, which were essential for the growth of democracy.

Abrogation of Democracy

It was in 1959 that Nepal was endowed with a democratic constitution and parliamentary government after the 1959 election. The Nepali Congress under the leadership of B.P. Koirala formed the government. But this system could not work for long. In December 1960 King Mahendra abrogated democracy and took power in his hands. In fact, King Mahendra had expressed, more than once, his dissatisfaction over the functioning of the Koirala government. King Mahendra's own justification of the steps taken by him was that it was done in order to save the people and the country. A few days before the royal takeover he said in a speech that "the fair name of democracy should never be permitted to be exploited to do evil rather than good to the people."[10] He had further made it clear that he too had certain responsibilities and he would not hesitate in taking steps in order to fulfill those responsibilities.[11] He alleged Koirala Ministry for failure in improving law and order situation in the country. He said that situation had compelled him to take steps in the interest of the people. However, it was in convincing that his concern for the deteriorating conditions of the country alone led him to the abrogation of the parliamentary system. In fact, what appears to be more logical is that he had distaste for the western style of democracy and did not want to see it developing in his own country. He had expressed his disliking for the parliamentary democracy as early as 1955. In a speech on 8th May, 1955, he said "... four round years have passed since democracy was brought in by the joint efforts of us all. During this period the government has been run by several cabinets of ministers... The balance sheet of profit and loss to the people from these various experiments is before the people.... concrete achievements could not be ensured from such a state of affairs."[12] In spite of his personal disliking for the western democratic system, King Mahendra could not take steps to immediately uprooting the democratic processes that had begun in the kingdom soon after the overthrow of 100 year old autocratic Rana rule in 1951. He had to keep the promise of his late father and thus, held parliamentary elections in 1959. King Mahendra had to accept people's verdict for the time being. But his ambitions and the lust for power ultimately compelled him to take a drastic step, such as, the abrogation of the infant parliamentary democracy. He was clear in his perception that if democracy would come to a stay in Nepal he would not be able to assert in politics.

Search for an Indigenous Democracy: The Panchayat System

After taking over powers, King Mahendra moved towards searching an alternative political order, which would establish supremacy of the Monarchy and at the same time, fulfill minimum democratic aspirations of the people of Nepal. With this objective he appointed a 'Constitution Committee' to study the political systems of some of the developing countries, like Pakistan, Indonesia, Egypt, Nigeria and Yugoslavia. These countries had established political systems claimed to be as the 'third world model of democracy'. It would be interesting to note here that in these countries the so-called alternative democratic political order was evolved by the rulers in order to legitimize their own authorities, such as, Ayoob Khan did in Pakistan, Sukarno in Indonesia and Nasser in Egypt.[13]

The underlined assumptions behind studying the politico-administrative institutions of these countries were stated to be that; *(i)* the western democracies had failed in the third world societies, therefore, such a political order was needed which would be based on the "cultural tradition and wisdom of the people of the third world countries," *(ii)* it was not possible to establish democracy by imposing it on people from the above. It should operate at the 'grass-root' level and develop upwards and *(iii)* in underdeveloped societies the political parties were obstacles in the evolution and development of the democratic institutions. Therefore, the political system should function without any formal political organization.

In order to realize these assumptions in their own country, the Constitution Committee suggested for the establishment of the 'Panchayat System', which obviously resembled Ayoob's 'Basic Democracy', Sukarna's 'guided democracy' and the 'class organisation' systems of Egypt and Yugoslavia.[14] The main features of the Panchayat system were; "party less" character of the polity, supremacy of the Monarchy and its guidance and control at all levels of the Panchayat organizations; decentralization of political power and class coordination. King Mahendra described the new political order as a truly 'Nepali' political system based on the culture and tradition of Nepal. Hence, it was an 'indigenous political order'.[15]

The Panchayat system provided for a four-tier hierarchical organization with the National Panchayat at the top followed by zonal, district and village or town Panchayat in the descending order. The representatives to the village or town panchayats, which formed lowest tier of the Panchayat system, were elected directly by the village or town assemblies constituted by the adult population of the villages or towns within its boundaries. Above to village or town panchayats the indirect method of election was in practice wherein the representatives of the lower tier elect representatives to the higher tiers of the panchayats.[16] The 1962 panchayat constitution also provided for a council of ministers headed by a Prime Minister appointed by the King. The council of ministers was an administrative body responsible for the implementation of the policies and programmes of His Majesty. The King was at the top of the system holding all the powers of a sovereign ruler. Every organization within the system was under his guidance and control. He was the repository of all legislative, executive and judicial powers. Apart from this, there were certain institutions that were formed with the objective of popularizing the Panchayat ideology in the countryside, and creating support for the Panchayat system under the active leadership of the king. Thus, a guidance council was formed to coordinate the activities of various class organizations. In 1967, 'Back to the Village National Campaign' (BVNC) was launched as an ideological move with a view to popularizing 'Panchayat Philosophy' in the countryside.[17]

The new political order was, however, not acceptable to the democratic forces of the kingdom. Hence Panchayat system had to function under heavy opposition from the outlawed political parties. Though the political parties or organizations were declared illegal in the new political set-up, they had remained a potent threat to the Panchayat system in the following years. Since the beginning, they demanded liberalization of the Panchayat system. Later on, such demands were also raised from within the Panchayat system. The working of the Panchayat system did not prove to be accommodative to the popular hopes and aspirations. It gave rise to dissatisfaction among the masses, especially, the students, who were annoyed with the policies of the government. The discontent of the people further grew as the government tried to consolidate the powers of monarchy instead of broadening the system and taking the people into confidence. It, however, ultimately brought the system at a turning point in the early months of 1979 when it was demanded to abolish the Panchayat system. It reflected that a large section of the people had lost confidence over the Panchayat system.

The Panchayat system was made to function without political parties or organized groups with political motives. It appears that the party less character was not as much the need of the Panchayat system, much as the personal liking of King Mahendra. He was of the opinion that political parties could function only in a developed society. In fact, it appears that the political parties were not allowed to function because they were considered as a threat to the position of the King. In Practice, however, the Panchayat system was faced with a serious lacuna. While it aimed at establishing democracy at the "grass root" level, it did not have any alternative mechanism to provide political education to the poor, illiterate and traditional people. Though, motives behind the formation of class organizations were to use them as substitute to political parties. However, class organizations were not allowed to participate in the organized political activities. It is a moot question whether any organization could fulfill political functions without having certain basic political rights. However, despite the ban on the political parties their activities could not be totally restrained and they indeed posed a perpetual threat to the Panchayat system from both within and outside the government.

The four-tier Panchayat organization though provided both, for a pattern or local government and a framework for the entire political set-up, it was faced with serious limitations. Panchayats were given the responsibility to popularize the ideals of the 'panchayat democracy' among the masses, and to act as channels of decentralization of the political power. However, in practice, such responsibilities were totally missing. The structures and powers of the panchayats were not in conformity to these responsibilities. The National panchayat which was the highest legislative body of the country did not have a truly representative character. Its members were elected indirectly. Out of a total 135 members of the National Panchayat, 23 members were king's nominees. The powers and functions of the National Panchayat were limited up to discussions on various issues and to make recommendations. On certain cases, like royal family, National panchayat had to take prior permission for a discussion on them in the house. The decentralization of powers in the panchayat hierarchies was missing in practice. At the levels of district and village or town panchayats there were parallel hierarchies of government officials, panchayat workers and the Back to the village National campaign officials. Therefore, there was utter confusion and often a conflicting situation regarding their powers and responsibilities.

It appears that the working of the panchayat system nearly for three decades could not change the traditional elite structure. In Nepal traditionally high caste, high education, higher economic status, and identification with the hill culture have been essential perquisites to enter into the power structure. Three hill communities, i.e., hill Brahmins, Kshatriyas and Newars have fulfilled these pre-requisites since the beginning. These three castes have been dominating the politics, administration and the army since the days of the Shah and the Rana rule. Their domination over the power structure continued during the 30 years of the panchayat system. This is evident from the fact that in the administration nearly 90 per cent of the higher posts were filled from among these three castes. As early as 1969 out of a total 290 positions above the under Secretary level 271 were occupied together by Chattris, Bhramins and Newars while they constituted 12.11 per cent, 6.0 per cent and 4.6 per cent of the total population respectively. The people of the Tarai occupied only 6 positions. In defense services out of 185 senior army officers in 1970, 137 were Chattris, 12 hill Brahmins and 12 Newars, 12 Gurungs and rest were other hill people. Only 1 person was from the Tarai. Similar trends were observed in the representative institutions. For example in 1967 in the National Panchayat Brahmins, Chettris and Newars had occupied 75 per cent of the total seats.[18] The people of the Tarai secured 10.4 per cent seats. In the National panchayat, they occupied 81 seats out of a total strength of 120 seats in 1975. The people of the Tarai secured 11.6 per cent seats only. This trend continued during the seventies and the eighties. These three castes not only dominated at the national level, but they also had domination in the district and village panchayats. It indicates that the panchayat system failed to broaden itself to the various communities and regions of the society. It continued to be based on the support of the traditional elite. Such disparities were, however, resented by the people of the Tarai region as well as the hill communities who did not have adequate representation in the bureaucracy and politics. They gradually became conscious about their neglected position. Such a political system was hardly expected to be people oriented.

The panchayat system also remained non-responsive to the popular aspirations and demands. Though both late King Mahendra and King Birendra claimed for more than once, that there were enough rooms for reforms in the panchayat system, in practice little thought was given to broaden the political system to the masses. Since the very inception of the panchayat system demands were being raised from the various quarters of the society for the liberalization of the political system, lifting ban on the political parties, holding direct elections to the panchayat organizations based on adult franchise and granting fundamental rights to the people etc. However, the Panchayat ruler conceded none of these demands, though the 1962 panchayat constitution had been amended for twice in 1967 and 1975. On the contrary, discernible attempts were made through these constitutional amendments to further consolidate the authoritarian tendencies.[19]

The most significant aspect of the 1975 constitutional amendment was the emergence of the 'Back to the Village National Campaign' (BVNC) as the most important institution in the panchayat system. The BVNC, which came into existence in 1967, as a non-constitutional body was, now with its nation-wide ramifications, culminated like a 'Politburo' of the panchayat system. Earlier, the idea behind forming the BVNC was to accelerate the pace of development activities in the rural areas thereby popularizing the ideals of the 'panchayat democracy' among the people. However, in the 1975 constitutional amendment, its role was totally altered and it was now given the responsibilities to act as an evaluator of the progress of the panchas and to recommend for reward or punishment to them by the Government. It was also entrusted with the task to maintain discipline and control among the panchas. The most important function of the BVNC was to recommend the candidature of a person seeking election to any of the panchayat organs. It was said that no person would be allowed to approach for election to the panchayat organs without approval of his candidature by the BVNC. Such provisions were, however, made in order to check the infiltration of the members of the banned political parties to the panchayat organizations, as well as, to restrain emergence of an alternative leadership.[20] In such circumstances, it was doubtful whether the BVNC could play a role of educating the masses. In fact apart from monarchical rhetoric, it did not give any evidence of being people oriented. On the contrary, its role alienated the people and the panchas from the politics. What made the BVNC most critical was the 'consensus method' adopted by it in the elections to the panchayat organs after the 1975 constitutional amendment? In order to exercise its powers regarding the guidance and control over the panchas, BVNC decided that the representatives to these institutions will be elected by arriving at a consensus among the electorate. However, in practice, BVNC imposed its choice and the so-called consensus over the electorate in the name of unanimity and integrity. It, obviously gave rise to discontent even among the panchayat cadres not to speak of the opposition groups because for them as well it became difficult to operate.

The panchayat system could also not provide a viable economic order to the country and the people based on equitable justice and social welfare. The economic conditions of the people had deteriorated severely under the panchayat system. The Economic Commission in a report submitted to the government in June, 1979 pointed out that "the economic conditions of Nepal were far from satisfactory." It observed that "the main causes for concern are declining agriculture productivity and failure to increase agriculture and industrial production. Lack of determination in revenue collection had led to deficit financing and increase in money supply." It further added that the discriminatory taxes on imports hindered the development of foreign trade. Particularly, the failure to increase exports to India had led to a serious trade deficit with that country. This only indicates that the Nepali economy had neither been able to boost up agriculture growth nor to streamline industrial development.

Thus, Nepali economy could not make any significant advance during the panchayat rule. There are evidences to indicate that the economic conditions remained unimproved during the various plan periods.[21] Nepal's the then Minister of state for Economic Affairs, Y.P. Pant in his budget speech for the year 1980- 81 stated that "the target envisaged in various sectors of the economy during the current plan (1975–80) have remained unfulfilled." The average population growth per year had remained 2.2 per cent and the GNP at 1.2 per cent. Out of the total 75 districts 45 were without any irrigation facilities. Nearly 94 per cent population was engaged in agricultural activities and most of them were under subsistence farming. The land structure had largely remained unchanged. The policies of the government aroused resentment among the farmers and other low income group people. They were annoyed of the exorbitant rate of revenue realized from the businessmen and the 'village and panchayat development tax' realized from the farmers. It was a burden for small farmers. Government's inability to provide essential commodities and the price rise also gave rise to discontent among the people.

The failure of the Panchayat system in broadening itself and meeting basic needs of the people gradually lead it towards a crisis. Interestingly at a time when the dissatisfaction was gradually brewing among the various sections of the Nepalese society, the return of Nepali Congress leaders, B.P. Koirala and Ganesh Man Singh, to Nepal in December 1976, after a long exile in India, was highly encouraging to the opposition.[22] It provided new hopes and strength to those who had been constantly demanding for the liberalization of the panchayat system. Soon after his return to Kathmandu, B.P. Koirala called for a national reconciliation with the King in favour of the Parliamentary system. He also called for a mass movement for the reestablishment of democracy in the country. It was since then the panchayat system was drowned into a crisis and ultimately to a serious jolt during 1979 mass movement.[23] King Birendra declared to hold a referendum in order to defuse the crisis in May 1980.

Many hopes were pinned on the May 1980 referendum which the country was to hold in order to decide whether to continue with the panchayat system or a change over to the multi-party system. The Nepali Congress and other parties of the Kingdom were much hopeful that the results of the referendum would go in their favour.[24] The Nepali Congress indeed was over enthusiastic about its performance and thought that it alone would be able to form the government independently after the results of referendum goes in favour of the multi-party system. However, to a great dismay of the political parties the results of the referendum went in favour of the continuation of the Panchayat system. Thus, the possibility to abandon the panchayat system through constitutional means got frustrated. The panchayat system was reformed in December 1980 though a third amendment to the 1962 constitution.

The attitude of the political parties towards the subsequent constitutional reforms, which provided for direct elections to the National Panchayat was not favourable. Their main objection was that it did not contain any practical measures towards the restoration of democracy in the Kingdom. The political parties did not participate in the 1981 elections once the plea that the political system did not provide congenial atmosphere for popular participation and political freedom and that the ban on political parties had continued.

In the 1986 elections to the National Panchayat, the Nepali Congress, despite strong resentment among the cadres, continued to follow the policy of electoral boycott. On the other hand, many of the outlawed political parties participated in the elections and registered a satisfactory performance. For instance, Communists secured 16 seats. Actually the Nepali Congress leadership was strongly divided over the issue of contesting the 1986 elections. One group was in favour of reconciliation with the King and believed that certain reforms could be introduced before the elections were held. But the other did not agree to it and wanted to boycott the elections. As a result, the party could not take a concrete decision early and a situation of indecisiveness and confusion prevailed for sometime. The Nepali Congress leaders were invited by the government to discuss the issue of freedom of speech, impartial atmosphere in elections, ban on political parties, etc., raised by it but the talks failed. The party's belated decision to keep itself away from the elections had resulted in revolt among its cadres who were in favour of participating in the elections. A number of party members decided to contest the elections independently. The party cadres were more frustrated because initially they had been instructed to prepare themselves for the election. Later on, the party could not launch a nationwide campaign to convince the people about its stand. It appears that party's decision to boycott elections could not exert much influence on voters, as, on an average, the voting turnout was 60 per cent.

On the contrary, the Nepali Congress policy to boycott elections had, in a way, provided strength to the panchayat system. It was thus clear that the party lacked a clear cut policy. It also became certain that there were differences among its leaders. There was no proper assessment of the strength and weakness of the party. It was feared that in the context of the growing dissatisfaction among cadres the party would further lose its support base. Keeping these developments in view the party decided to participate in the 1987 local Panchayat elections. But its performance was quite dismal.

It can be said that the 1980 reforms in the panchayat system also failed in providing a responsible government and a broad based system. On the contrary it gave way more problems to the panchayat system itself.

Thus, it can be said that the panchayat system failed in realizing popular aspirations and needs. It also did not provide any alternative to western model of democracy. It remained a facade of democracy. It indeed provided a democratic cover to the absolute rule of the monarchy. Nepal's search for a third world model of democracy proved to be a failure, as it could not gain popular support. The developmental issues remain un-addressed and opposition to the system continued throughout.

Concluding Observations

The modern Nepal came into existence through a process of military expeditions by the rulers of the Gurkha principality. The evolution of the Nepali political system is characterized by authoritarian monarchic rule, feudalistic socio-economic order, upper caste domination on the positions of power and authority, religious identity of the monarchy, hill cultural domination over the Tarai region, synonimity of the institution of monarchy and the Rana rulers later on, with the state, intrigues and palace conspiracies, rewards and punishment, isolationalism and backwardness. These factors gave a peculiar character to the Nepali political system in which despotism, domination, disbelieve, lack of confidence, dissonance, opposition and fear became the main issues. All these issues have important bearings upon the contemporary politics of Nepal.

The tyrannical rule of the Ranas invited opposition and strong resentment among the people. However, the Rana rulers tried their best to see that the anti-Rana movement does not gain any base in Nepal. The movement took an organizational shape in India. But as they tried to launch an armed struggle against the Ranas from the Nepali soil it came to an abrupt end.

The restoration of the powers of the monarchy also opened avenues for the growth of democracy in Nepal. But Nepal's exposure to democracy was quite sudden and without any preparedness on the part of the traditional elite, democratic elite or the masses. It seems that the whole process was full of contradictions. There were political parties looking for the democratic governance in the country. There was the monarchy delighted with the restoration of its powers. Than there were the Rana rulers representing the feudal class who were still being offered a share in the power structure. In these circumstances where was the scope for democracy? Moreover, the ground realities were that the political parties lacked a social base and political experience, society was backward and feudal to the core and there was no economic infrastructure in the country so as to meet the aspirations and expectations of the people.

The argument of the monarchy was that the western model of democracy was not suitable to the Nepali conditions. Hence, there was a need for an indigenous model of democracy. But it also did not prove fruit bearing. The panchayat system, which was introduced as a third world model of democracy also failed. Actually the monarchy was not prepared to give-up its political authority and there was a class who had vested in the perpetuation of the monarchic authority. Because it was under the leadership of the monarchy that they enjoyed their hold over bureaucracy, politics and economy. It is because of the vested interest of this class that sufficient socio-economic base could not be build for the working of democracy.

Nevertheless, the democratic instincts of the Nepalese remained alive even during the era of panchayat rule for two reasons. Firstly, because the Nepali ruling elite adopted a dualistic postures. The monarchy assumed supreme political powers under the panchayat system but also created a facade of democracy. So even if the political parties and organized politics were not operative, political parties remained alive and active in different ways. Secondly, the monarchy adopted contradictory policies. After 1950, the monarchy assumed the role of a modernizing agent. Though political reforms and liberalization was restrained socio-economic modernization was allowed. The people of Nepal came in contact with the outer world.

Gradually a small middle class began to emerge in Nepal, which was educated, ascriptive and modern in outlook. They desired political liberalization along with economic development, the aspirations of the rising middle class coincided with the political motives of the outlawed political parties and that gave a way for a popular movement against the panchayat rule.

REFERENCES

1. For a detailed understanding of the geography see, H.B. Gurung, "The Geographical Foundations of Nepal", The Himalayan Review, 1(1), 1969; P.P. Karan, Nepal, A Physical and Cultural Geography, Kentucky, 1960.
2. Bhuwan Lal Joshi and Leo E. Rose, *Democratic Innovations in Nepal, A case of Political Acculturation*, California University Press, 1966: 3.
3. For an account of the different phases of history of Nepal the following works are useful. E.B. Hamilton, *An Account of the Kingdom of Nepal*, Edinburgh, 1819; H.B. Hudson, *Essays on the Language, Literature and Religion of Nepal and Tibet*, Manjushri Publication House, New Delhi, 1972; *Daniel Wright, History of Nepal*, Calcutta, 1955; Toni Hagen, Nepal: The Kingdom in the Himalayas, Kummerly and Fray, Berne, 1961; Ludwing F. Stiller, *The Rise of the House of Gurkha*, Manjushri, New Delhi, 1973; D.R. Regmi, *Modern Nepal*, Firma K.L. Mukhopadhyay, Calcutta, 1961; Ram Niwas Pandey, *Making of Modern Nepal*, Nirala, Delhi, 1997.
4. See for details, Anirudh Gupta, *Politics in Nepal*, Bombay, 1964.
5. For a study of the Rana Political system see, M.S. Jain, *Emergence of a New Aristocracy in Nepal*, Sri Ram Mehra & Company, Agra, 1972; Adrian Server, Nepal Under the Ranas, Oxford & IBH, New Delhi, 1993.
6. See, K.M. Majumdar, *Nepal and the Indian National Movement*, Firma, K.L. Mukhopadhya, Calcutta, 1975.
7. For details see, Bhuwan Lal Joshi and Leo E. Rose, N. 2.
8. India played a significant role in bringing up this agreement and helped Nepal subsequently in framing the constitution. See K. P. Karunakaran, India in World Affairs 1950-53, Oxford University Press, Delhi, 1958: 124; Bhola Chatterji, *A Study of Recent Nepali Politics*, World Press, Calcutta, 1967.
9. Anirudh Gupta, N. 4: 155.
10. H.M. King Mahendra, *Proclamations, Speeches and Messages*, HMG, Kathmandu, 1967; Pt.2.

11. Bhola Chatterji, *Nepal's Experiment with Democracy*, New Delhi, 1977: 99–100.
12. Proclamations .... N. 10.
13. See, Margret W. Fisher and Leo E. Rose, *The Politics of Nepal: Persistance and Change in an Asian Monarchy*, Cornell University Press; Ithaca, 1971.
14. N. 13: 52.
15. Bhuwan Lal Joshi and Leo E. Rose, N. 4.
16. For details see, Rishikesh Shaha, *Nepali Politics, Retrospect and Prospect*, Oxford University Press, New Delhi, 1978.
17. For details of the working of the Panchayat system see, Borgh Erik Borgstrom, *The Patron and the Panka*, Vikas, Delhi, 1980.
18. Fredric H. Gaige, *Regionalism and National Unity in Nepal*, Berkeley 1975: 169.
19. See, L.S. Baral, "Changing Constitutional and Political System of Nepal", *Foreign Affairs Report*, January, 1977.
20. B.C. Upreti, "Back to the Village National Campaign: An Estimate", *Centre for the study of Nepal*, BHU, Varanasi, March, 1979; Rishikesh Sha, N. 16.
21. B.C. Upreti, "Nepal's Budget in a Difficult year", Eastern Economist, August, 1980: 532.
22. B.C. Upreti, "Nepal's Panchayat Democracy in Nepal", *Eastern Economist*, January 25, 1980: 187.
23. See for the post-1980 Panchayat Politics, Rishikesh Shah, *Politics in Nepal 1980-90*, Mahohar, Delhi, 1990.
24. See, D.P. Kumar, *Nepal: A Year of Decision*, Vikas, Delhi, 1980.

3

Breaking the Path: The 1990 Democratic Movement

The beginning of the decade of 1990's proved to be a turning point in the recent political history of Nepal. The democratic forces of the kingdom got united after a long gap of 30 years and posed a challenge to the panchayat system. It was indeed not an easy task because of two reasons. The democratic forces were not allowed to operate in an organized form within the panchayat system. Secondly, the panchayat system was considered to be a highly powerful form of governance under the overall leadership of the king. The 1990 mass movement succeeded in reestablishing the democracy in the kingdom. The understanding between different political parties to come together and to launch a united struggle against the panchayat autocracy was a significant headway in this regard. Earlier in 1980, the political parties had failed in reaching to such an understanding, as a result of which they lost in the 1980 referendum.[1] So what lead to the polarization of the political groups is an important issue. What were the other factors and events that contributed to the growth of the democratic movement? What were the considerations that compelled king Birendra to decide for the abrogation of the panchayat system? To what extent the 1990 movement was a successful movement? These are some of the issues that are being addressed to in this chapter.

Struggle for Democracy: The Backdrop

The panchayat system that came in operation in 1962 established a party less political system and all the existing political parties and organized political activities were legally banned. King Mahendra also tried to bargain with the democratic political leaders. Many of them left their parties and joined the panchayat system. The political parties were demoralized and they became dysfunctional. However, the individual party leaders did not give up their political fights and continued their struggle in their individual capacity. They continued to demand for the reforms in the panchayat system, lifting ban on political parties and restoration of democracy in the kingdom. Some of the communist parties and groups started underground political activities. They paid more attention to strengthening of their bases and the grooming of party cadres. Some of the communist parties opened the party offices outside the country and continued their activities against the panchayat system. Thus the panchayat system could not uproot the political parties though their activities were constitutionally banned. Actually, the political parties were considered to be the main source of threat to the absolute powers of the monarchy. It is a fact that the panchayat system was installed in the country just to provide a democratic cover to the rule of the king. Thus it was a façade of democracy. The non-participatory character of the panchayats, party less ness and non-existence of popular dissent clearly reflected upon the nature and dynamics of the panchayat system. But the point is whether it was possible to abolish the political parties from the political scene of the country once they had been operative for a decade? In fact, it was an unimaginative and undemocratic consideration of the panchayat leaders to ignore the existence of political parties in the country for which it had to pay.

The panchayat system faced opposition from the banned political parties continuously. It became more pronounced after 1969, when many of the democratic political leaders began to demand for representation in the panchayats.[2] The first serious movement against the policies of the panchayat government broke out in 1973-74 represented by youth and peasants. But instead of liberalization of the panchayat order attempts were made to further consolidate the system in the second amendment to the panchayat constitution in 1975. The constitutional amendment failed in satisfying the democratic forces.

The return of Veteran Nepali Congress leaders, B.P. Koirala and Ganesh Man Singh to Kathmandu in 1976 gave a new strength and momentum to the democratic forces to start a nation wide movement against the panchayat system. The movement actually began in 1979 as a student agitation but soon other political forces joined it and it took a wider shape and started demanding establishment of a multi-party system in place of the panchayat system.[3]

King Birendra declared to hold a referendum in May 1980.[4] The democratic forces withdrew the movement but they lost in the referendum. Apart from the fact that the panchayat camp enjoyed support of the powerful monarchy and also that the governmental machinery was obviously in the lands of the panchayat leaders. The democratic forces lacked unity.[5] In fact, it was none less than Nepali Congress supremo B.P. Koirala who declined a communist proposal to come to a common platform to fight against the panchayat system in the referendum. Koirala suggested that let all the political parties campaign for the multi-party democracy individually. It was a tactical mistake on the part of the political parties. They did not realize the ground situation that did not favour them. The parties like Nepali Congress were over confident regarding its position. The parties had to pay for that and they lost an opportunity to bring back the multi-party democracy in the country.

Cracks within Panchayat System

The panchayat system though got a verdict in the referendum in favour of its continuation. Some developments took place during the eighties which indicated that differences were occurring inside the panchayat system and it was heading towards groupism, rivalries and oppositional politics. It may be noted here that the monarchy wanted to keep panchayat system away from its politicization and political fragmentation. But now things were undergoing a change, particularly after the third amendment in the panchayat constitution towards the end of 1980. The amendment provided for selection of the Prime Minister by the national panchayat. This lead to the growth of group politics within the panchayat system, some thing that was unusual for it's profounder. The developments that followed clearly indicated that the panchayat system was gradually loosing its grip.[6] The divisions and splits were gradually brewing up in the ranks of the panchayat supporters. After the 1986 election to the national panchayat, some of the panchas started demanding reforms in the panchayat system. Some of the panchas also demanded resignation of their own Prime Minister. This clearly indicates that the panchayat system was loosing its solidarity. There was lot of corruption taking place. On the other hand, the banned political parties were continuously opposing the panchayat system. There were clear indications that the panchayat system was moving towards a difficult situation due to its own problems, as well.[7]

Polarization of Democratic Forces

The polarization of the democratic forces of the kingdom at various levels towards the end of the eighties and the beginning of the nineties was the most significant development that took the very foundation of the panchayat system. The communist parties of the kingdom took a lead in this regard. A United Left Front (ULF) was constituted by Nepal Communist Party (Manandhar), Nepal Communist Party (Varma), Nepal Communist Party (Amatya) Fourth Convention, Nepal Workers and Peasants Organization (Rohit), etc. Initially there were nine communist groups but later on these remained seven. In January 1990, the United Front decided to form a United Communist Party called United Marxist Leninist party (UML). The Nepali Congress agreed to form a joint front with the UML. There had been a long history of mutual distrust and non-cooperation between the Nepali Congress and the Communist Parties. But the realization that it was not possible to pose a formidable challenge to the panchayat system without coming together succeeded in bridging their differences. There was a realization that it was not possible to overthrow the panchayat system by constitutional means. The Nepali Congress leadership realized the need for a united struggle for democracy after its humiliating defeat in the 1987 local panchayat elections. Taking all these circumstances into consideration, the Nepali Congress and the ULF decided to launch a movement for democracy in the country. Mohan Bikram Singh and Pushpa Kamal Dahal also decided to join the movement against the panchayat system.

Regional Context

There were two important developments in the region, which had high significance for the struggle for democracy in Nepal. At the first place the Indo-Nepal imbroglio of 1988-89 brought down the prestige of the panchayat system and underlined its failure in managing the affairs. The dead-lock in India-Nepal relations towards the end of the decade of the eighties, the expiry of the trade and transit treaties between the two countries and the subsequent strained relations between the neighbours was largely due to the misperceived notions of the leaders of the two countries towards each other. But than the economic hardships that the people of Nepal faced following the expiry of the trade treaties brought in the perception that the panchayat leadership was not concerned to the problems of the masses. The Nepali Congress and the communists tried their best to in cash the situation in their favour. They propagated that the panchayat leaders alone were responsible for the failure in negotiating with India. Thus just on the eve of the democratic movement the panchayat leadership faced a set back, carried a derogatory impression about its diplomatic maneuvering and its non-concern towards the people's sufferings.

Another regional development that is worth mentioning here is the changes taking place in the domestic politics of some of the countries of the region. India was heading towards a significant political change while in Bangladesh and Pakistan circumstances were getting favour to a democratic political order in these countries. This was a moral boosting development for the democratic forces of Nepal and a demoralizing change of events for the panchayat leadership, as they would loose the regional backing for its authoritarian rule if democracy were to come to these countries.

Support of Indian Political Leaders

It was for the first time that the Indian political leaders in their capacity of representatives of the political parties and in their individual capacity lend their support and encouragement to the democratic forces of the kingdom. Though the Government of India did not, at any stage, tried to lend its support to democratic political forces but the way political leaders like Chandra Sekhar and other socialists supported the Nepali Congress leaders in their efforts to launch a movement clearly indicated that there was a considerable support and sympathy among the people of India towards the movement in Nepal. Chandra Sekhar joined the Nepali Congress convention and called for a mass movement against the autocratic regime. His presence proved to be a great moral support to the Nepali Congress leaders.[8]

International Context

Interestingly the international political environment was also building in favour of democratic regimes since the beginning of the decade of eighties. There was a world-wide emphasis in favour of liberalization and democratization of political regimes. The communist regimes of Eastern Europe were succumbing to democratic forces one after the other. It gave an impression that it was not impossible to remove the strong authoritarian regimes as well. This was naturally an encouraging development for the democratic forces of Nepal.

Social Organizations and Groups

An important development that had taken place in the late 1970's and 1980's was the formation of various social organizations and their assertions in respective fields, despite the control of the panchayat government on the organized activities. It was towards the end of the 1970's that the various Mongolian ethnic groups began to organize them and come to a common platform. They were though, not clear about their goals and possible course of action at this stage, it was a significant development as a deprived, dissatisfied and marginalized section of the Nepali society was trying to unite itself. It also gave impression of the rise of ethnicity in Nepal in the course of time. The Human Rights Organizations had also come up and they were raising voices against the atrocities of the panchayat government. Apart from this, the students, various organizations of professionals like advocates, teachers, journalists, doctors, etc., were also coming up. It was indicative of social transformations taking in Nepali society at one level and the discontent taking an organized shape at the other level.

The various organizations that took a significant part in the movement later were Democratic National Unity Forum, Nepal Students Federation, All Nepal National Independent Students Federation, Ex-Servicemen of the British and Indian Armies, Nepali Goodwill Council, People's Front, National Worker's Organization of Nepal, Nepal Trade Union Centre, Organizations of Teachers, Advocates and medical practioners and SETA MAGURALI (Sherpa, Tamang, Magar, Gurung, Rai, Limbu Organisations).

Objectives of the Movement

What was the perception of the joint front and what did they want is an important issue here. It was clear in the minds of the democratic forces that the panchayat system was undemocratic in nature and therefore it had to be abolished. They were also clear that it was not possible to replace the panchayat system throw constitutional means for two reasons. There was no scope within the panchayat system for the political parties to operate. Secondly, the existing panchayat order best suited to the political interests of the king and hence he was not prepared to reform the panchayat system beyond what had already been done. So, the only alternative was to launch a nationwide movement.

The democratic forces wanted that the ban on their activities be lifted. They also wanted to replace the panchayat system by a multi-party democracy where the power rests in their hands that they get the opportunity to contest elections based on the principle of adults franchise and to form a government under a new constitution.

The democratic forces were not against the king. They only wanted that the powers of the king be taken away. But no harm be done to the institution of monarchy. The monarchy be preserved as an institution of social and religious importance and as a symbol of national unity and integrity. They were against the panchayat system because it had institutionalized the powers of the king.[9] It was clear that the democratic forces were against neither the absolutist rule of the king nor the institution of monarchy. This clearly reflects upon the perception of the democratic forces regarding the possible future political scenario of the kingdom.

Beginning of the Movement

The beginning of the movement for the restoration of democracy in the Kingdom may be treated the 18 January, 1990 national convention of the Nepali Congress. It was the first convention of the Nepali Congress party in last 10 years that received a nation-wide consideration. It was considered to be a powerful show by any political party for the first time in last many years.[10] Prior to the convention, speaking in a meeting, the Nepali Congress President K.P. Bhattarai had said:

> "Today a new wave of democracy and freedom is sweeping the world. Despotic and dictatorial regimes have become islands in the ocean of the free world and their days are numbered. This is true of Nepal as well. Even senior leaders of panchayat system are now admitting publicly that the system has achieved nothing. The impact of the deadlock in Indo-Nepal relations has proved how hollow the claims of development made by the panchayat system are."

He further state that:

> "The Nepali Congress remains committed to the goal of full democracy and human rights in Nepal. We have convened this conference to decide on the character and date of a nation-wide peaceful movement aimed at the liquidation of the present party less or one party system."[11]

The Nepali Congress convention posed a clear challenge to the panchayat government and also it indicated a determination of the democratic forces to start a nation-wide struggle for the establishment of democracy. The event was naturally disturbing to the panchayat government. The panchayat leaders also tried to demonstrate its strength. Public meetings, rallies and processions were organized all over the country. On 18 January, 1990 a mass rally was organized in Kathmandu. The government with its wide spread canvassing was expecting a huge turn out. But it proved to be a failure as there was not much mass support to the rally.[12] The veteran panchayat leaders like Surya Bahadur Thapa and Rajeshwar Devkota did not attend the rally.[13] It clearly revealed that there were internal disputes in the panchayat leadership. The events clearly indicated that:

1. The democratic forces were in a processing consolidation and were preparing for a movement.
2. The panchayat leaders were aware of the situation and so they were trying to reconsolidate themselves.
3. It was becoming clear that the panchayat system was loosing mass support.

Chronology of Events

The democratic movement was formally commenced on 18 February, 1990. The public demonstrations, strikes and confrontation with the government officials took place in many parts of the country. The government took immediate measures to contain the movement. Censorship was imposed on media. A large number of political leaders were locked up. The Communists through their underground network tried to generate mass support for the movement. The atrocities of the panchayat government converted Nepal into a police state. Despite the government suppression there was a steady increase in the movement. The movement also became violent. A number of associations such as Medical Association, Bar Association, Teachers Association joined the movement and it became widespread.

The situation underwent a drastic change when movement started in Bhaktapur. Not only that it became intensive but also took a violent turn. Bhaktapur indeed played a significant role in bringing the democratic movement to new heights.[14] An agitation in the Tribhuwan University campus in Kathmandu was yet another turning point. In fact, it took the democratic movement to its climax.[15]

Interestingly, at a time when the democratic movement was spreading in and outside the Kathmandu valley king Birendra was out of the capital city. He had camped at Pokhara and was busy in visiting different parts of western Nepal, as if he was not aware of what was happening in Kathmandu. He was surrounded by a close group of his associates. At a time when the government was in much need of his support and guidance the king left the government alone and took its own decision. It was indeed difficult for the Prime Minister to act efficiently in such a situation. It is believed that Nepali Congress leader K.P. Bhattarai who was under house arrest had suggested the king that he could stop further violence and the emerging anarchic situation by declaring a reform package while addressing a panchayat rally at Pokhara on 16 March, 1990.[16] But the king did not utilize this opportunity to announce any reforms.

The movement reached to its climax between 1–9 April, 1990.[17] The Foreign Affairs Minister of Nepal S.K. Upadhyay resigned in protest against the repressive measures taken by the Government. Meanwhile, the government employees, officials of the Royal Nepal Airlines and civil servants also began to support the movement. The panchayat system had already lost people's sympathy. On 2 April, the cabinet was reshuffled.

On 6th April Lokendra Bahadur Chand was appointed as the Prime Minister of Nepal. It was decided to start a dialogue with the political parties. King said to the Prime Minister, if the leaders of the Nepali Congress have clear ideas about political reforms, you should start a dialogue with them."[18] But no dialogues could take place between the government and the political parties because of fast developments taking place within the panchayat system. Lokendra Bahadur Chand was forced to resign and Marich Man Shrestha was brought in as Prime Minister. But again Lokendra Bahadur Chand replaced him. This also demoralized the government.

On 7th April Tundikhal Parade took place in Kathmandu. Curfew was imposed in the city. But people became unruly. The king broke its long silence and declared lifting of ban on the political parties on 8th April and dissolved the government. He said in an announcement:

> "Respect for the ideals and values of democracy have always guided us in the conduct of the affairs of state. It was in this spirit that we held a referendum in 1980 to allow the people to choose the kind of changes they wanted in the polity of the country. It is the government's duty also to maintain law and order. Regrettably, since the present council of ministers has not been able to do so, resulting in the loss of life and property, we have in consonance with the popular will and in accordance with the constitution of Nepal, dissolved the present council of ministers.....[19]

On 16 April king announced dissolution of the National Panchayat, Panchayat Policy and Evaluation Committee and 6 class organisations.[20]

This brought an end to the democratic movement and also to the panchayat system. But interestingly, it was the king who emerged as the main actor in the final show and not the joint front of the political parties. It is also interesting to note that the king laid all blames for atrocities, failures and misconduct on the panchayat government and did not share any responsibility with the panchayat government. Ultimately, he got sided with the people and in his own explanation did what the people of Nepal wanted. The democratic forces accepted the outcome and for nothing the king became the hero of the movement.

Reasons for Success of the Movement

We have already made it clear that the 1990 democratic movement was an outcome of several factors. We would just like to recapitulate some of the points for the purpose of analysis of the events. Let us first look at it from a different angle as to why did the panchayat system failed? It seems that apart from being undemocratic, unresponsive, authoritarian and narrow in nature the panchayat system had proved to be contradictory in its approach. In fact, one would say that the panchayat leadership ignored the ground realities. After 1960 lot of developments were taking place in education, infrastructural and economic fields. There was lot of increase in the social and political awareness of the people. The panchayat system failed in changing itself in accordance to these changes taking place in the Nepali society. On the contrary it did not allow liberal reforms in the politics of the country. As a result of these contradictions it failed in gaining popular support and sympathy when the system was in much need of it.

The political parties realized the need for consolidated efforts to be made against the panchayat regime. Their efforts were strengthened and supported by the changing regional and international environment. There was a local dissatisfaction among the industrialists, traders and businessmen due to trade embargo with India.

The growth of ethno–regional consciousness also went against the panchayat system. The people of Mongolian communities had already expressed their dissatisfaction on the eve of the 1980 referendum. They were trying to organize themselves since then in order to preserve their socio-economic and political interests. In Bhaktapur and Patan Newar identity broke against the panchayat system. In the Tarai region people were highly dissatisfied on the issue of citizenship, their meager political representation, etc.

The students and various professional groups were also dissatisfied with the policies of the panchayat system. The provisions of the class organizations and the 'Go to the Village National Campaign' had failed in creating a sound basis for the panchayat system.

On the whole it can be said that the 1990 democratic movement was a broad based socio-political movement having a nation-wide and in depth support base.

A Comparison of 1950 and 1990 Movements

The 1950 movement was against the Rana rule and the movement was organized in the Indian soil and than began in Nepal. It also aimed at establishing a democratic system in the country. Interestingly, many of the political leaders who had participated in the 1950 movement were supreme leaders of the 1990 movement.

The two movements bear some similarities and some differences. Both the movements came to an abrupt end at a time when they had reached to their climax. As a result of it the outcome of both the movements was a compromised one. Both the movements paved way for a political change in the country. But could not bring any fundamental change in the socio-political fabric of the country. In both the 1950 and 1990 movements the outcome rested around securing the interest of the institution of monarchy and the traditional political elite.

However, the 1990 movement was much more widespread in comparison to the 1950 movement. The 1990 movement received an unprecedented mass support.[21] It can be said that the 1990 movement made a little headway in terms of the political set-up of the country and installed the constitutional monarchy.

Concluding Observations

The 1990 movement for democracy was path breaking in the sense that it brought an end to the panchayat system for the time to come. It also opened doors of the country to democracy. But it has proved to be half won battle on many counts.

The king very clearly brought an end to the movement by declaring abrogation of the panchayat system. Perhaps he was apprehending that if the movement continues further it could go against the monarchy as well. So before any harm could happen to the political interests of the king he got the situation altered. The political parties accepted the king's declaration and withdrew the movement without realizing the fact that there was no understanding reached between the two groups over the future course of politics in Nepal. Why did political parties accept king's declaration and got the movement off without any negotiated settlement? Did they fear that the movement might run out of their hands? Were they becoming impatient to hold on to power or there was a truce between political parties and the king? The reason must be somewhere near to these factors.

But the point is that the future course of events clearly indicates that perhaps there was a tactical flaw on the part of the political parties. They should have clearly defined the goals of the movement according to the minds of the people not in terms of their political interests. Similarly the movement should have been brought to an end on their own terms and conditions. The king laid all blames on the panchayat system and himself became the protector of the mass aspirations and the political parties just clapped on this. Than why such a big movement was raised?

The political parties had to pay for it very soon. They were ill represented in the Constitution Committee and hardly had much say in the new constitution. The traditional political elite still remain dominant and the course of politics surrounded the monarchy not the democratic political parties in the subsequent years.

REFERENCES

1. See, B.C. Upreti, "Politics of referendum in Nepal" in M.D. Dharamdasani (ed.), *Political Participation and change in South Asia,* Varanasi, 1984: 24-63.
2. For a discussion of these issue, see, Lok Raj Baral, *Oppositional Politics in Nepal,* New Delhi, 1977.
3. D.P. Kumar, *Nepal, A Year of Decision*, Vikas, Delhi, 1980.
4. B.C. Upreti, "Nepal's Panchayat Democracy in Crisis." *Eastern Economist,* January 25, 1987: 187.
5. For details see, Lok Raj Baral, *Nepal's Politics of Referendum,* Vikas, Delhi, 1983.
6. Martin Hoften, *et.al., People, Politics and Ideology, Democracy and Social change in Nepal,* Mandala Book Point, Kathmandu, 1999-115.
7. See for details, Rishikesh Shaha, *Politics in Nepal,* 1980-90, Manohar, Delhi, 1990.
8. B.C. Upreti, *The Nepali Congress,* Nirala Publications, New Delhi, 1983: 23–40.
9. Martin Hoftern, "The Dynamics and Chronology of 1990 Movement' in Michael Hutt (ed.), *Nepal in Nineties,* Oxford University Press, Delhi, 1994: 15.
10. Michael Hutt, N. 9: 17.
11. Rashtra Pukar (Kathmandu), January 18, 1990; also see *Nepal Press Digest* (Kathmandu), Vol. 34, No.4, January 22, 1990.
12. Dristi: (Kathmandu), January 29, 1990.
13. Michael Hutt, N. 9: 17.
14. Dhanendra Purush Dhakal, *Jan Andolan* (Nepali) Kathmandu, 1990.
15. T. Louise Brown, *The Challenge to Democracy in Nepal: A Political History,* Routledge, London, 1966: 122.
16. Rishikesh Shah, N. 7: 196.
17. Martin Hoften, N. 6: 128.
18. Ogura Kiyoko, *Kathmandu Spring: The People's Movement of 1990,* Himal Books, Kathmandu, 2001: 159.
19. *Gorkhapatra* (Nepali, Kathmandu), April, 7, 1990.
20. Ogura Kiyoko, N. 18: 153.

4

Structural Foundations of Democracy

The promulgation of democracy itself is not sufficient. It has to be promoted, strengthened and institutionalized. The long-term sustenance of democracy depends on its structural foundations. In fact, there are two important aspects relating to the working of democracy in any country. Firstly, it requires institutional arrangements and structures that give a double foundation to democracy. Secondly, the operationalisation of democracy takes place on the basis of foundational provisions.[1] There are close interlinkages between the two. The operationalisation of democracy dependence on the sound basis of democratic structures, and the strong and appropriate democratic structures open ways for the proper functioning of democracy. A proper coordination between the two leads to the institutionalization of democracy. In many of the third world countries democracy failed or over powered by the authoritarian rulers because it lacked strong structural foundations. So the success or failure of democracy depends considerably, on the structures that have been created in the country for the operationalisation of the system.

This chapter seeks to discuss various structural foundations, which were laid in the kingdom following the April 1990 declaration of King Birendra. It also focuses upon the formation of governments and the political process that represents both structures and operationalisation of democracy.

The Coalition Government

After the abolition of the panchayat system the question of formation of an interim government came up, which would run the administration of the country till a popularly elected government could take up its place. To let the panchayat government continue as an interim government was not feasible, as it had become very unpopular among the masses. Moreover, the political parties would not have accepted it for obvious reasons. At the same time, the King himself would not have been allowed to hold powers as an interim provision because that could have given rise to suspicions about the motives of monarchy. Therefore, a coalition government of the Nepali Congress and various factions of the communists formed the government under the leadership of the Nepali Congress leader K.P. Bhattarai. It may be recalled here that the communist factions and the Nepali Congress had formed a joint morcha to fight for the restoration of democracy in Nepal. The coalition government consisted of four ministers of the Nepali Congress, three of the Joint Left Front, two nominees of the King, and two intellectuals.[2] It was decided that the ministry would be further expanded at some appropriate time in order to accommodate four constituents of the United Left Front who had so far not been given a place in the ministry.[3]

The coalition government had two major tasks to complete: to promulgate a new constitution for the country based on the principles of constitutional monarchy and than to hold elections. The coalition government came into power at a time when the country was facing a deep economic crisis, largely due to the impasse in Indo-Nepalese relations two years back. Therefore, it was expected that the government would provide some immediate economic relief to the people. Nevertheless, its political tasks were of primary importance as the future of democracy in the Kingdom depended on the successful completion of the above mentioned two tasks. There can be no doubt that the Bhattarai government completed its duties successfully. Despite many odds the coalition government remained in power almost for a year. It is surprising that the two ideologically opposed political parties could run the governments till the end. In fact, the Nepali Congress as well as the communist factions was committed to the restoration of democracy in the Kingdom, and it was clear that the breaking of coalition government would disrupt the whole process. Also, an important factor was that both the Nepali Congress and the communists had contributed in the movement almost equally and both were aspiring to form government individually after winning in the general elections. Hence, they did not want to be labelled as disruptor of the movement by not cooperating in the coalition government. Thus, the coalition of the Nepali Congress and the UML worked not for positive reasons that much but for to avoiding the negative connotations of breaking the coalition. No doubt that the successful working of the coalition government was a very difficult task which K.P. Bhattarai completed skillfully. The communists themselves were divided and there were seven factions of communists in the United Left Front and it was not an easy task to keep them intact in the government[4]. However, the coalition government could not register any significant contribution in the field of socio-economic reconstruction and development. Thus, the immediate economic relief that the common people were aspiring from the Bhattarai Government remained unfulfilled.

THE CONSTITUTIONAL APPARATUS

The constitution is the basic structural foundation for any democracy to operate. It reflects upon the kind of governmental system a country is going to adopt. It also reflects upon the desires and aspirations of the people and the ways and means it follows for their realization. Two issues are important relating to the constitution and its implication for the working of democracy: who provides the constitution? and what are the perception and attitude of the constitution committee?

The formation of a new constitution in order to replace the 1962 Panchayat constitution was the first major requirement for the operationalization of democracy in Nepal. A Constitution Recommendation Commission was constituted for this purpose by King Birendra in May 1990, headed by Justice Bishwanath Upadhyay of the Supreme Court.[5] The objective of the Commission was stated to be to recommend for the establishment of constitutional monarchy and multi-party democracy "in the interest of Nepal and the well-being of the Nepali people."[6] Thus, the focus of the Constitution Recommendation Committee had to be on the constitutional monarchy. Hence, it did not have many options.

The formation of the constitution committee, however, aroused a lot of criticism. The Nepali Congress was not happy with the inclusion of some of the members in the committee. The government was not consulted before formation of the committee so it was also an issue of resentment. G.P. Koirala strongly resented this fact.[7] He said in a statement thus:

> "The Nepali Congress feels that the Constitution Commission has been formed in a manner contrary to the spirit of constitutional monarchy under the multi-party system. It appeals to HM to reconstitute the Commission in consultation with the interim government"....[8]

In fact, the interim government wanted that it should be properly consulted in the making of the constitution committee. It was because of strong resentment against the commission that King Birendra dissolved it on May 15, 1990. He accordingly directed the Prime Minister to recommend names for a new commission in consultation with the council of ministers and political parties.[9] Thus, a new commission was formed. However, the process of constitution making remained controversial. The issue was whether the Commission should prepare the constitution or it should be done by an elected Constituent Assembly. Some of the Communist parties demanded that a Constituent Assembly be constituted for this purpose. The Communist Party of Nepal (Mashal) threatened to launch a movement in this regard.[10] The United National People's Forum started a series of demonstrations and public meetings in order to mobilize people in favour of the formation of a Constituent Assembly.[11] The Communist Party of Nepal (Adhikari) had rejected the idea of formation of a Constituent Assembly but stressed upon the fact that the commission should consist of the representatives of the United Left Parties and the Nepali Congress.[12] Man Mohan Adhikari objected to the commission being called Constitution Recommendation Commission.[13] The Nepali Congress did not subscribe to the view of the formation of Constituent Assembly. The Nepali Congress Supremo, Ganesh Man Singh strongly condemned such a demand. He opined thus:

> "How can we believe that the demand for a constituent assembly, which had not been made during the movement, is not intended to disrupt the general elections? If the intention behind such demand is good, why are not efforts being made to have such matters incorporated in the new constitution? It is certainly not necessary to follow a path, which may nullify the gains of the movement."[14]

It seems that the parties that had played a major role in the 1990 movement were desperately looking for a share in the power structure of the country and they were not in favour of loosing time. It also appears that in the circumstances prevailing in Nepal at that time, the formation of a Constituent Assembly would have been a time-consuming process. Also, there were suspicions regarding the role and motives of the Palace. Therefore, the main political parties did not support it.

The constitution making itself was a difficult process. So many opinions and doubts were expressed regarding its nature and pattern. In fact, it was a tribute to the political acumen of K.P. Bhattarai that the constitution was, however, promulgated. He had played a crucial role in this regard. He made all efforts to build a consensus between the Royal Palace and the council of ministers regarding the provisions of the constitution.

Main Features of 1990 Constitution

King Birendra promulgated the new constitution of Nepal on 9th November, 1990. It envisaged for a constitutional monarchy in the kingdom.

The Constitution has following main features:

I. The Constitution declares Nepal a multi-ethnic, multi-lingual, democratic, independent, indivisible, sovereign, Hindu and constitutional monarchical Kingdom. The sovereignty vests in the people of Nepal. The objective of the constitution is stated to be to consolidate adult franchise, parliamentary system, constitutional monarchy and multi-party system "by promoting amongst the people of Nepal, the spirit of fraternity and the bond of unity on the basis of liberty and equality."[15]

II. The Constitution provides for fundamental rights to the people. Reasonable restrictions are also laid down upon these rights in the general interest of the public. Special provisions have been made to protect interests of women, children, physically or mentally handicapped or aged persons and economically and socially backward people. The fundamental rights are applicable to all without any distinction of sex, caste or creed. These rights are quite extensive. The main rights provided in the constitution are: right to equality, right to freedom, press and publication right, right regarding criminal justice, right against preventive detention, right to information, right to property, cultural and educational right, right to religion, right against exploitation, right against exile, right to privacy and right to constitutional remedy.[16] The fundamental rights have further been substantiated by the provision of the directive principles of state policy.

III. The Constitution provides a constitutional status to the monarchy. The King is a titular head of the state. The institution of monarchy has been regarded as a "symbol of the nation and the unity of the Nepalese people."[17] His Majesty is exempted from property and income tax and no question can be raised against him in the court.

IV. The powers of the executive vest in the King and these shall be exercised by a council of ministers headed by the Prime Minister, except those powers, which are exclusively vested in the His Majesty. It provides that the Prime Minister will be the leader of the majority party in the House of Representatives. The concept of collective responsibility has been accepted.

V. The Constitution envisages for a bicameral legislature, namely the House of Representatives and the National Council. The membership of the House of Representatives is 205 elected on the basis of universal adult franchise. Its term is 5 years, which can be extended for a year under special circumstances. The National Council has sixty members of whom 10 are nominated by the King, 35 including two women members to be elected by the House of Representatives on the basis of proportional representation by means of the single transferable vote, and 15 members to be elected at the ratio of three members from each of the five development regions. The National Council is a permanent house and one-third of its members shall retire every two years. Their tenure will be six years. The constitution states that the membership of any house will cease if a member deserts the party on whose ticket he has won the election. The legislature has no right to discuss issues related to the royal family.

VI. An independent judicial system is envisaged in the constitution. The judicial system will have three-tiers: the Supreme Court, the appellate courts, and the district courts. A Judicial Council has also been constituted to recommend principles regarding the appointment of the judges and the other judicial functionaries. All the judges are to be appointed by His Majesty on the recommendation of the council of ministers.

VII. The Constitution makes provisions for the formation of a number of institutions like the Raj Parishad, Auditor General, Election Commission, Abuse of Authority Investigation Commission and Public Service Commission.

VIII. According to a provision of the constitution all the political parties of the Kingdom are required to register with the Election Commission. In order to get recognition of the Election Commission each party must have five per cent women candidates and should obtain, at least, three per cent of the total vote cast in the House of Representatives. It has specifically been mentioned in the constitution that no law can be passed to banish or put restrictions on the political parties. This provision has been made keeping in view the Panchayat System in which political parties were not allowed to function. No political party based on religion and ethnicities are allowed to contest elections.

IX. The emergency provisions vest with the monarchy. It has been said that in case of external aggression, internal armed revolt or extreme economic depression, which threatens sovereignty and integrity of the country or the security of any part of the Kingdom, the King may declare a state of emergency. Such a declaration will have to be approved within three months by a two-third majority of the House of Representatives. In case such a declaration is approved it shall remain effective for six months from the date of its first announcement. It can be extended maximum to another six months by a majority of two-third members present in the house. In case it is not approved, the declaration shall immediately cease to be effective. The fundamental rights will remain suspended during the state of emergency.

X. The Constitution also provides for a Defence Council consisting of the Prime Minister, the Defence Minister, and the Commander-in-Chief. The council has been entrusted with the task of administration of army and looking after the defence matters.

XI. The Constitution can be amended by a two-third majority in each house of the parliament. But the amendment in any article of the constitution or its repeal cannot change the spirit of the constitution as reflected in its preamble.

It is clear from these provisions of the constitution that it has provided for the establishment of a parliamentary system of the British or the Japanese type. The constitution is almost similar to the 1959 constitution, but is totally opposed to the 1962 panchayat constitution in which sovereignty had vested in the King who held the supreme political powers. Thus, the promulgation of the 1990 constitution was an important landmark towards the establishment of democracy in Nepal.

ELECTORAL PROCESS AND POLITICAL REPRESENTATION

General elections at a fixed interval as provided by the constitution, is a primary indicator of the working of a democratic political system. The general elections on a regular interval provide yet another important structural foundation of democracy.

Elections ensure involvement of people, groups and parties at various levels, in the political system. It provides an opportunity to the people to exercise their right to vote and select their representatives. Elections are an opportunity through which people can influence the decision-making of the government.[18] In fact, general elections are an opportunity through which responsibility and accountability of the political leaders can be assured. It can be said that general elections are a means of collective decision-making process and voting is the most significant means of popular participation in this process.[19]

It is believed that in a democratic system power must rest with the people. It is through the provision of universal adult franchise that the people exercise this power.[20] Thus, it can be said that the periodical general elections are the nerve system of a democratic political order. A democratic system cannot function without elections based on universal adult franchise and held on a regular interval.

Like all democratic systems the 1991 constitution also provided for general elections based on the principle of universal adult franchise on a regular basis. The constitution also defined rules and regulations relating to the formation of election commission and rules and regulations relating to general elections.

Delimitation of Constituencies and Election Procedures

It was necessary to redefine constituencies and divide the whole country in various parliamentary constituencies. In this connection the constitution has provided that the 75 administrative districts of the Kingdom shall be deemed to be the election districts. It was decided to allocate seats to each district on the basis of its population according to the latest census report. It is ensured in the constitution that each district is allocated at least one seat irrespective of its population.

A three member Constituency Delimitation Commission was also constituted according to the provision of the constitution. The Commission was entrusted with the task of determining the number of seats from each district for election to the House of Representatives and than delimit the constituencies for the districts having more than one seat. It was expected that the Commission while delimiting the constituencies should take into consideration the boundaries of the administrative districts, geographical factors, density of population, transportation facilities and the ethnic composition of the area in terms of homogeneity or heterogeneity. It has been provided in the constitution that no question shall be raised regarding the delimitation of constituencies in the court of law. The whole country has been divided into 205 parliamentary constituencies.

Voting Right

The election to the House of Representatives has to be held on the basis of 'one man one vote' through secret ballot. The constitution provides that any citizen of Nepal attaining the age of 18 years shall be entitled to vote. Thus the principle of universal adult franchise has been adopted.

The Election Commission

Detailed provisions have been made for the formation of an Election Commission headed by a Chief Election Commissioner and other Election Commissioners appointed by His Majesty.

The powers and duties of the Election Commissioners have been stated as conducting, supervising, directing and controlling elections to the parliament and other local bodies. The Election Commission has also been empowered to take a final decision regarding the disqualification of a member of parliament. It has also been pointed out in the constitution that the Election Commission will perform such duties and functions as laid down by law from time-to-time.

Legal Provisions

Steps were taken by the Bhattarai Government to make necessary legal provisions in order to conduct the general elections scheduled for 12th May, 1991. Three acts were promulgated to provide the necessary legal framework to prepare for elections. They were: the Member Representation Act, the Election Commission Act, and the Election Crisis and Offences Act.

Features of 1991 Elections

The 1991 general elections were unique in certain respects. These elections were supposed to be the trend setters as it were the first under the auspices of the 1990 constitution.

I. The time period in which general elections were held in Nepal was of specific importance. Not only that the political environment of the Kingdom was undergoing a change after the success of 1990 movement for democracy, but the whole region (South Asia) was in a state of political transformation. Pakistan and Bangladesh had witnessed elections and India was going for elections along with the elections in Nepal.

II. The foreign policy issues were important in the elections from the Nepalese point of view. The one-and-a-half year impasse in Indo-Nepalese relations had proved to be disastrous to the country. The Nepalese economy had received a serious jolt because of disruptions in the supply of essential commodities from India.[21] At the level of domestic politics the paradoxical alignment of centrists with leftists was rather an ambiguous situation. It was difficult to believe that such an alignment would ensure democracy and stability. It rather depended on the outcome of the elections.

III. The elections were significant because of the lowering down of voting age from 21 to 18 years. The younger generation was to cast vote for the first time in these elections. It was estimated that there will be an overwhelming increase in the number of voters. Along with this change, these elections to be held under a constitutional order ensuring a multiparty democracy had made it a 'critical election' representing socio-political changes in the country.[22]

IV. The 1991 elections were in a way characterized by an upsurge of ethno-regionalism in Nepal. It is a fact that there had been a strong resentment among some communities and regions because of discriminatory policies followed against them by the panchayat system. The discontent among these communities remained latent so long as the panchayat system was in operation due to the lack of political rights and the fear of suppression by the Government. But as the situation changed after April 1990, there was a sudden upsurge of these forces. The various mountainous communities of Tibeto-Mongloid origin like, Sherpa, Tamang, Gurung, Magar, Rai, Limbu, and so on, felt that they were not given proper representation in the politico-administrative structure of the country. Therefore, just before elections they formed a separate party representing their interests.

The problem of Madhesias was more serious. While the Tarai region has been economically prosperous the people of Tarai never received proper representation in the administration, politics and military structure of the country. Besides, they had been demanding a status of official language to Hindi. The Nepal Sadbhavana Party took up the task of fighting for the causes of Madhesias. The party had raised citizenship, linguistic and regional issues and demanded formation of the autonomous region of Tarai. It should be made clear that the issues raised by these parties were of fundamental nature from the point of view of cementing national unity and integrity.

V. One important feature of these elections was that the whole electoral process was marked by a clear-cut contest between progressive forces who were in favour of democracy, stability and development and the obscurantist who wanted to re-establish traditional values.

VI. The issues like political freedom, political rights, democracy, multi-party etc., were not present in this election, as they had been in the elections under the Panchayat system because this election was to held in a democratic constitutional framework. However, the major issue appeared to be whether people should vote for traditionalists, generally represented by two National Democratic Parties or for political reformists represented by Nepali Congress and radicals who would like to further change the system. The regionalists point of view represented particularly by Nepal Sadbhavana Party was also important.

VII. Another important feature of these elections was that there was hardly any wave in favour of any of the political parties that were contesting in the general elections.

VIII. It is interesting to note that except the Nepali Congress which had claimed to win the elections since the beginning, none of the political parties claimed to score majority seats in the elections. The general speculations of these parties were that a coalition government would emerge after the elections.

IX. The inter-party allegations and counter allegations were important in the electoral campaign. The issue often raised was that the Nepali Congress had links with India, which the Nepali Congress strongly denied. But such issues did not affect much the outcome of the 1991 general elections.

It is clear that the 1991 general elections were important in many respects and it was likely to be a trendsetter for the future course of democracy in the country.

Electoral Issues and Campaign

Out of the 40 political parties registered with the Election Commission 22 political parties filed nominations in the elections. The Nepali Congress was the only political party that had nominated candidates for all the 205 seats. The UML, second largest political party had 177 candidates. National Democratic Party (Thapa) and National Democratic Party (Chand) had 163 and 154 candidates each. 219 independent candidates also fought the elections. There were 1,11 42,638 voters in the 1991 general elections out of which nearly half were women voters.[23]

The political parties raised different issues and programmes in their manifestos. The Nepali Congress stressed on democratic socialism as its fundamental objective. The party also emphasized prosperity of people and the nation, human dignity, socio-economic parity, development of rural areas, decentralization, equal opportunities to people and world peace.

The UML on the other hand, emphasized planned economic development and pledged its struggle against economic disparities, exploitation and corruption. The party also talked of a balanced regional development, introduction of land reforms, protection of rights of poor farmers and labourers. On the foreign policy issues it advocated equal relationship with India and China, revolution of all treaties and agreements signed by previous governments that were unequal, disadvantageous and derogatory to Nepal. National Democratic Party (Thapa) pledged its support to the constitutional monarchy and multi-party system. The party projected itself as an alternative democratic party that had to play a leading role in the politics of Nepal.[24] National Democratic Party (Chand) on the other hand, entered the election fray with the slogan that 'Let us save the nation, reconstruct it and safeguard democracy.'[25] The party supported constitutional monarchy, mixed economy free education to all up to the secondary standard, heavy industries and close relations with the two neighbours. The Communist Party of Nepal (Amatya) called for the initiation of popular national democracy, heavy industrialization special treatment to labourers, depressed castes and tribal people. It supported equal relationship with India and China.

The Dalit Mazdoor Kissan Party affirmed its commitment to the creation of an equalitarian society based on democracy, secularism and socialism.[26] Janata Dal (Socialist-Democratic) emphasized up on its struggle for the creation of a socialist democracy.[27] Rashtriya Janata Dal (H) gave the slogan of 'removal of poverty.'[28] While Nepal Rashtriya Jana Mukti Morcha called for democratic socialism and local autonomy.

Nepal Sadbhavana Party being a representative of Tarai concentrated on the problems of the Tarai region. The party strongly reacted to the discrimination against the people of Tarai.[29] It demanded proper representation of Tarai in the politico-administrative structures of the country, inclusion of Hindi as an official language and abolition of discriminatory policies based on language, region and ethnicity.

There were certain common issues that came up in the manifestos of most of the political parties. The socialist path of development was supported by most of the parties. Similarly constitutional monarchy, multi-party democracy, mixed economy, etc., were highlighted in the manifestos of most of the parties. The issues relating to political stability and good governance, development of natural resources, national security, etc., were not given importance in the manifestos of different political parties.

The election campaign of different political parties was marked by intra–party and inter–party differences and rivalries. There was more emphasis on personal attacks and abuses than concentrating on national issues. None of the political parties agreed for electoral alliance. Their election strategies and campaigning clearly reflected lack of electoral experience and powerful leadership. The major political parties were more interested in raising issues relating to relations with India, while these issues were not those important for the elections.[30]

The total voting turnout in the 1991 general elections was 65.15 per cent. The voting percentage was higher in the Kathmandu Valley (75%) and some part of the Tarai region. Only 4.4 per cent votes were invalid, which was not a big number keeping in view the low literacy rate and poor voting experience of the people of the country.

The Nepali Congress with 110 seats emerged as the winning party though with a razor thin majority. It secured 39.50 per cent of the total valid votes. The UML emerged as the main opposition party with 69 seats and it got 29.27 per cent of the valid votes in its favour. The other parties which got an entry to the lower house of the parliament were National Democratic Party (Chand), 03, National Democratic Party (Thapa) 01, Joint People's Front 09, Nepal Sadbhavana Party 06, Communist Party of Nepal (Democratic) 02, Nepal Workers and Peasants Party 02 and Independents 03. It clearly shows that the political parties that have a background of being panchayat supports were almost rejected by the voters. In contrast, the JDF had a better performance, which emerged as the third largest party in the lower house with 9 seats. The independent candidates were also rejected by the voters as only 3 out of 259 could find their way to the parliament. Perhaps it was realized that the question of strengthening democracy and political stability was prime to Nepal and the independents could have contributed a little to this.

It is interesting to note that many of the party stalwarts belonging to the Nepali Congress as well as to some of the other political parties lost the election.[31] The Nepali Congress lost eight of ten seats of the Kathmandu valley. The Nepali Congress registered a better performance in the Tarai region as it secured more than 63 per cent seats there. The Kathmandu valley, eastern region emerged as the UML strong holds, while Nepali Congress dominated the western region. The 1991 general elections set the trend that the Nepali Congress and the UML were the two major political parties of the kingdom.

1994 Mid-term Elections

The 1991 general elections paved the way for a weak government and a strong opposition. But more than the weak position of the government, the intra-party disputes of the Nepali Congress and the leadership conflicts soon came to the surface, making it almost impossible for the government to run the administration. The Nepali Congress Party was sharply decided along organizational and government lines represented by K.P. Bhattarai the party president and G.P. Koirala the Prime Minister. The UML took advantage of the NC factional politics and joined hands with the dissatisfied group of the NC, which was prepared to the extent of going against its own party's government.

It became almost impossible for Prime Minister G.P. Koirala to run the government due to the opposition by its own party members. On 10 July, 1994, Koirala resigned and recommended dissolution of the parliament. The parliament was dissolved by the king and mid-term elections were declared for 13 November, 1994. It aroused lot of controversy. The anti–Koirala group of NC did not like Koirala's action, while Koirala pointed out that if the Prime Minister were to be removed from the office on the personal wishes of an individual a stable government was not possible. A faction of the Nepali Congress demanded action by the Party against the Prime Minister.[32] It was suggested that the Nepali Congress and the UML should jointly boycott the mid-term polls.[33]

The UML appreciated Koirala's resignation but did not favour dissolution of the lower house. The other communist parties also viewed King's action unparliamentary and undemocratic.[34] However, the two national democratic parties and Nepal Sadbhavana Party welcomed the decision of the monarchy.

Thus the political parties were divided on the issue of holding early polls. However, the events leading to the mid–term polls were indicative of certain emerging trends of Nepali politics:

1. It became clear that the task of political stability and continuity was difficult in Nepal due to intra-party conflicts.
2. It was also evident that the socio-political conditions were not yet much supportive to the process of institutionalization of democracy in the country.
3. The democratic leadership was more concerned about its own prospects of holding the power rather to the long-term prospects of democracy, stability and development in Nepal.

In 1994 mid-term elections 55 political parties applied for the registration with the National Election Commission. 44 political parties were given recognition. The Election Commission recognized 5 political parties as national parties. There were altogether 24 political parties in the elections.

Electoral Issues, Plans and Projections

The different political parties emphasized upon their future plans and policies in the manifestos issued by them. The Nepali Congress again emphasized upon the policy of democratic socialism and pleaded that the basis of democratic socialism was socio-economic justice. It was possible to fight against hunger, poverty, disease illiteracy, injustice and exploitation by adopting democratic socialism.[35] The party emphasized that there was a need to increase the production and the employment opportunities. The party supported liberalization and privatization. The party also emphasized upon safe drinking water facilities, abolition of dual ownership of land, promotion of Nepal's image as a peaceful and democratic country and peaceful relationship with all countries on the basis of mutual cooperation and equality.

The UML party assured that it would provide a clean, healthy and efficient administration. The other aspects that were emphasized by the party in its manifesto were: promotion and protection of the multi–party democracy, eradication of irregularities and corruption, proper utilization of revenues and foreign assistance, reduction of foreign debt, steps towards laying foundation of an independent economy, increase in agriculture production, securing forest resources, socio-economic equality, planned development, land reforms and reorganization of agriculture sector, poverty alleviation through increased avenues of employment in the agriculture sector and friendly relations with all the countries on the basis of non-alignment and principles of panchsheel.[36]

The Communist Party of Nepal (Marxist) reiterated its commitment to nationalism and rights of the people. The party called for the abrogation of all international treaties. It also emphasized upon converting Guthi land into Raikar land, land to landless farmers and minimum wages to farmers and labourers.

The National Democratic Party declared its commitment to nationalism, democracy and the constitution. The party also laid its commitment to land reforms, reconstruction of rural economy, population control, etc.

Nepal Mazdoor and Kishan Party criticized the use of money in elections. It called for a struggle against price rise and improving the conditions of workers and peasants. The party viewed elections as a class struggle and that her efforts would be to raise workers and peasants to the status of ruling class.[37]

Nepal Sadbhavana Party pledged its support to constitutional monarchy, federal system, religious freedom, constitutional rights and duties. It demanded that 50 per cent places be reserved for Tarai and 30 per cent for hills.[38]

It is clear from an overview of the manifestos and electoral declarations of the major political parties that there were a number of common issues that were supported by all. For instance, constitutional monarchy, multi-party democracy, rural reconstruction, restructuring land system, etc., were raised by most of the political parties. In the 1994 general elections there was a more focus on the socio-economic issues, particularly the problems relating to socio-economic transformations. However, in the electoral campaign and meetings the political leaders concentrated more on attacking the leaders of the rival parties.

Electoral Performance and Outcome

It is interesting to note that out of 24 political parties 19 parties failed in securing a single seat in the house of representative. The total votes polled in the 1994 elections were 62 per cent. Thus the percentage of voting had lowered down in comparison to 1991 elections. The outcome of the mid-term polls was not at all encouraging as none of the political parties could secure majority. There was a close contest between UML and Nepali Congress. However, UML became the largest party in the House of Representatives with 88 seats, followed by Nepali Congress with 83 seats. UML secured 42.93 per cent votes and Nepali Congress 40.49 per cent. The position of other parties was National Democratic Party 20, Nepal peasants and Workers Party 4, Nepal Sadbhavana Party 3 and Independents 7. There was a marginal increase in the number of independent candidates. The National Democratic Party also emerged as a gainer as it had a benefit of 16 seats over the previous position. There can be no doubt that the Nepali Congress had to pay for its infightings and leadership clashes. It had a loss of 27 seats over the 1991 elections.

The UML continued to dominate the hill region and the Nepali Congress the Tarai region, although there was a decrease in the performance of Nepali Congress in the Tarai in comparison to the 1991 elections.

1999 General Elections

The 1999 general elections were important for various reasons. It was for the first time that elections were held in two phases: 3rd May and 17th May, 1999. It was alleged in some quarters that such a provision made by the Election Commission was against the provisions of the constitution. The Election Commission, however, argued that such a provision was made due to security reasons, as it required lot of security arrangements to hold elections at a time. It appears that in the context of the ongoing Maoist terrorist activities in some parts of the countries, disturbances were being apprehended in the elections. Hence, it required lot of security arrangements. In these elections voter's identity card system was introduced in Kathmandu, Bhaktpur, Lalitpur-2, Sunsari-1 and Baitadi-1, constituencies on an experiment basis. A total 2427 persons filed nominations out of which 1647 candidates belonged to 42 political parties and 780 were independent candidates. 203 candidates withdrew from the candidature, the final position thereby remaining to 1605 candidates belonging to 41 political parties and 619 independents.

The Nepali Congress was the only political party that put candidates for all the 205 seats of the lower house. The position of other political parties was: UML 194, CPN-ML 198, National Democratic Party 197, National Democratic Party (Chand) 184, Nepal Sadbhavana Party 68, National People's Liberation Front 55, Hariyali Party 45, Nepal Farmer's and Peasants Party 41, National People's Council 39, People's Liberation Party 28, Nepal Backward

Labour Party 22 and Nepal Communist Part (United) 19, Thirteen Political Parties had put one candidate each.[39] It shows that the contest was basically between five political parties in terms of the number of candidates and between two political parties viz. Nepali Congress and the UML for their wide social bases.

Electoral Issues and Outcome

None of the political parties contesting the elections appeared into any electoral alliance or understanding and each party decided to contest the elections independently on its own. It may be pointed out here that the smaller political parties could have made such electoral alliances with the major political parties in accordance with their ideological parities. But, it seems that the main contenders were looking forward for its victory so that it could form government on its own. On the other hand, the small parties were not serious about their electoral performances. The fact that more than a dozen parties nominated one candidate each itself speaks of their seriousness in the elections. Perhaps, they only wanted to preserve their existence as a political party. Moreover, most of the smaller parties did not have any regional basis from where they could be considered as potential winners. Such a situation left the political parties to contest elections without any alliance or arrangement of seats. It is strange that the political parties had agreed to form coalition governments later on but not for the electoral alliance at the time of general elections. It shows that most of the parties believed in power sharing rather in ideological commitment and the institutionalization of democracy.

The nomination process reflected upon internal party fluids and groupism. The Nepali Congress had to revise its list of candidates several times under the pressure of contending groups within the party. The factionalism within Nepali Congress is well-known and the party had to pay for it in 1994. However, one positive factor with the party was that despite factionalism and leadership clashes it had so far succeeded in keeping itself united. The party leadership also showed its ability to crisis management. After a peak situation of conflict the party could attain a normal position every time.

The UML was in a disadvantageous position. The party was faced with leadership clashes and groupism. In December 1997 it faced a serious set back when the radical group within the party got fragmented and formed CPN (ML). Thus, the party's strength was divided. At a time when the election campaign was at its peak UML chairman, Man Mohan Adhikari passed away, which also adversely affected the party. Both UML and ML appeared in the elections on the basis of a divided popular base. The National Democratic Party was also divided into two groups each claiming a separate status of the party yet depending upon the same social base. The Maoist groups had decided to boycott the elections and the threats given by the Maoist insurgents was a matter of concern for the government, the political parties and the voters.

As far the issues and promises are concerned most of the political parties stressed on good governance, clean administration, social justice, popular rights and development. The Nepali Congress continued to advocate its policy of democratic socialism. The National Democratic Party stressed upon Liberalization.

Another issue, which was emphasized by the major political parties, was welfare of the tribal communities and depressed classes. Reconstruction of rural economy, unemployment, poverty eradication, development of agriculture and industries were other issues touched upon by most of the parties. The ML talked of Nepal's equal share and equal rights in the sharing of river waters, revision of 1950 treaty of peace and friendship with India, resolution of Kalapani dispute etc. However, the political parties refrained themselves from making anti-Indianism as an issue in the elections, as it happened in 1994 mid-term elections.

It may, however, be pointed out here that inter-party allegations became more prominent during the campaign and election speeches of party leaders. The electoral meetings and campaign lacked an emphasis on the national issues and problems.

The issues that were important for the consideration of the Nepalese voters were political stability, democracy and development. The frequent changes in the government had questioned the strengthening of democracy in the country. It had also created a crisis of governability and the process of development was hampered. But, these issues were hardly raised in the electoral campaign. On the whole, one could observe that during the campaign there were fewer talks about major issues and problems and more inter-party attacks. It may also be noted that the leaders and parties gave more emphasis to personal contacts and door to door campaign.

Except the small posters and the leaf lets, no big posters and cut outs were used in the campaign.

Electoral Outcome and Performance

The voting took place for 201 seats and it had to be withheld on 4 seats due to the death of candidates in these constituencies. The Nepali Congress won 110 seats and secured majority in the house. The UML secured 67 seats, National Democratic Party 11, Sadbhavana Party 5, National People's Front 5, Nepal Peasants and Workers Party and United People's Front one each and rest were independents.

Six political parties got the status of a national political party. But unfortunately two of them were without wining a single seat in the general elections. According to the constitution of Nepal any political party, which gains 3 per cent votes in the elections to the parliament is recognized as a national party. The CPN (ML) could not secure even a single seat while it had contest on 198 seats. Similarly National Democratic Party (Chand) also failed in getting entry to the parliament. But they became national political parties.

A look at the statistics of elections reveals that the Nepali Congress gained seats in all the parts of the country but the important point is that it could win in some of those areas such as Jhapa, Ilam, etc., that were earlier considered to be the strong holds of the communists. The UML continued its dominance in the Kathmandu Valley. The Nepali Congress secured 36.3 per cent of popular votes. The UML secured 30.75 per cent. The National Democratic Party emerged as the third largest party with a popular base of 10.5 per cent votes. It may be pointed out here that in 1994 the undivided National Democratic Party had secured 17.93 per cent of the votes with 20 seats, which means that the social base of NDP had lowered down in this election may be due to the division in the party.

Strange enough was the situation of NDP (Chand) and CPN (ML) which could not secure a single seat in the house but got the recognition of a national party as they secured more than 3 per cent popular votes. While NPF and NPWP that secured 5 seats and one seat each, could not gain the status of a national party as none of them could secure 3 per cent votes.

One may also observe disparity between the popular votes won by a particular party and the number of seats won by it in the House of Representatives. The larger parties had greater number of seats in the house compared to their popular votes while the smaller parties had lesser number of seats comparing to their popular votes. Thus, the Nepali Congress won 54.73 per cent of seats in the house, while wining only 36.30 per cent of popular votes. The UML was 33.83 per cent seats and 30.75 per cent of popular votes. NDP secured 5.47 per cent of seats but 10 per cent of popular votes. The ML and NDP (Chand) together secured nearly 10 per cent of popular votes but no seats.

The electoral outcome of the 1999 general elections suggested that the people of Nepal had reiterated their faith in the Parliamentary democracy. Earlier, it was being apprehended that the Nepalese people were fed up with democracy. But now it appeared that they still look forward for democracy, stability and good governance in the Kingdom. They had seen fate of coalition governments and realized that governmental stability was the primary condition for development and realization of basic needs of the people.

It can also be said that the Nepalese voters had rejected the extremist ideology of whatever kind. The fact that the CPN (ML) and NDP (Chand) could not secure a seat was a witness to this kind of trend. It may be noted here that probably the communist voters did not like division within the UML as ML could not gain a seat even in areas of its strong hold. The political parties that voiced anti-Indianism also failed in joining any sympathy from the voters. The Nepali Congress formed the government after the elections.

Table–I
Number of Voters in Different Elections

Total Voters	*1991*	*%*	*1994*	*%*	*Change*
Total votes polled	11191777	100.0	12296219	100	+110442 0.1%
Invalid votes	322023	4.42	241071	3.16	1.26

(Contd.)

Total	*1999*	*%*	*% Change 1991*	*% Change 1999*
Total votes polled	13491831	100	2300054 20.5	1195612
Invalid votes	384739	4.40	.38	1.24

Source: Documents of the Election Commission, HMG, Nepal.

Table–II
Party-wise Performance in 1991 Elections

Name of the Parties	*Total Candidates*	*Seat Won*	*% of Total Seats*	*Votes Received*	*% of votes polled*
Nepali Congress	204	110	53.66	2752452	37.75
NCP (UML)	177	69	33.66	2040102	27.98
UPF	70	9	4.39	351904	4.83
NSP	75	6	2.92	298610	4.10
RPP (Chand)	154	3	1.46	478604	6.56
RPP (Thapa)	163	1	0.49	392499	5.38
NCP (Democratic)	75	2	0.98	177323	2.43
NMKP	30	2	0.98	91335	1.25
NRIM	50			34509	0.47
NCP	6			2562	0.04
JD (SP)	15			5760	0.08
AP	1			94	0.00
RIPN	9			4280	0.06
BJD	1			2012	0.03
NCP (BURMA)	35			16698	0.23
IMN	14			1518	0.02
NCP (AAMATYA)	15			4846	0.07
NRJP	4			5732	0.08
RJP (H)	27			4406	0.06
DMKP	1			92	0.00
Independents	219	3	1.46	303723	4.17
	1126	205	98.54	6969061	95.58

Source: Documents of the Election Commission, HMG, Nepal.

Table–III
Party Position in the House of Representatives, 1994 (Total Seats–205)

Name of the Party	*Seats won*	*Percentage of the Seats*
Nepal Communist Party United Marxist Leninist (NCP-UML)	88	42.93%
Nepali Congress (NC)	83	40.49%
Rastriya Prajatantra Party (RPP)	20	9.76%
Nepal Peasants & Workers Party (NPWP)	4	1.95%
Nepal Sadbhavana Party (NSP)	3	1.46%
Independents	7	3.41%

(Out of 24 political parties 19 parties in the fray have not been able to secure a single seat in the House of Representatives. SJM lost all 49 seats it contested).

Source: Documents of the Election Commission, HMG, Nepal.

Table–IV
Party Positions in the 1999 General Elections

S.No.	*Parties*	*Seat Won*
1.	Nepali Congress	111
2.	UML	71
3.	National Democratic Party	11
4.	Nepal Sadbhavana Party	05
5.	Nepal Workers and Peasants Party	01
6.	Rashtriya Jana Morcha	05
7.	Samyukta Jana Morcha	01
		205

Source: Documents of the Election Commission, HMG, Nepal.

Table–V
Changing Performance of Political Parties in Three Elections

Party	*1991 2048*	*1994 2051*	*Change*	*1999*	*Change 1991*	*Change 1994*
Rastriya Prajatantra Party	4	20	+16	11	+7	-5
Communist Party of Nepal (Democratic)	2	0	-2	Nil	0	0
Independent	3	7	+4	Nil	0	0
Nepali Congress	110	83	-27	111	+1	+28
Nepal Sadbhavana Party	6	3	-3	05	-1	+2
Nepal Workers and Peasants Party	2	4	+2	01	-1	-3
Communist Party of Nepal (UML)	69	88	+19	71	+2	-17
United People's Front	9	0	-9	–	–	–
Rashtriya Jana Morcha				05	–	–
Samyukta Jana Morcha				01	–	–
Total	205	205		205		

Source: Documents of the Election Commission, HMG, Nepal.

Table–VI
Shifts in the Base of Political Parties in Different Elections

Sl.	*District*	*Con-stituency*	*1991 Win-ner*	*1991 Run-ner*	*1994 Win-ner*	*1994 Run-ner*	*1999 Win-ner*	*1999 Run-ner*
1	*2*	*3*	*4*	*5*	*6*	*7*	*8*	*9*
EDR								
1.	Taplejung	1	UML	NC	NC	UML	UML	NC
		2	UML	RPP(C)	ML	RPP	UML	RPP
2.	Panchthar	1	UML	NC	NC	UML	UML	NC
		2	UML	RPP(C)	RPP(C)	UML	UML	NC
3.	Illam	1	UML	NC	UML	NC	NC	UML
		2	UML	NC	NC	UML	UML	NC

(Contd.)

1	*2*	*3*	*4*	*5*	*6*	*7*	*8*	*9*
4.	Jhapa	1	UML	NC	UML	NC	NC	UML
		2	UML	NC	ML	NC	UML	NC
		3	UML	NC	ML	NC	NC	UML
		4	UML	NC	NC	UML	NC	UML
		5	UML	NC	NC	NC	UML	NC
		6	UML	NC	UML	NC	UML	NC
5.	Sankhuwasabha	1	UML	NC	UML	NC	NC	UML
		2	UML	NC	UML	NC	UML	NC
6.	Tehrathum	1	UML	RPP(T)	ML	RPP	UML	NC
		2	UML	NC				
7.	Bhojpur	1	UML	NC	ML	NC	UML	NC
		2	UML	NC	ML	NC	UML	NC
		3	UML	NC				
8.	Dhankuta	1	UML	NC	ML	RPP	UML	NC
		2	UML	RPP(T)	RPP(T)	UML	RPP	UML
9.	Morang	1	NC	UML	NC	UML	NC	UML
		2	UML	NC	UML	NC	UML	NC
		3	UML	NC	NC	UML	UML	NC
		4	UML	NC	UML	NC	UML	NC
		5	NC	UML	ML	NC	NC	UML
		6	NC	UML	UML	NC	NC	UML
10.	Sunsari	1	UML	NC	UML	NC	UML	NC
		2	NC	UML	NC	UML	NC	UML
		3	NC	UML	NC	UML	NC	RPP
		4	NC	UML	NC	UML	NC	UML
11.	Solukhumlu	1	NC	UML	NC	RPP	NC	UML
12.	Khatang	1	UML	NC	ML	NC	NC	UML
		2	UML	NC	ML	NC	NC	UML
		3	UML	NC				
13.	Okhaldunga	1	NC	UML	NC	UML	NC	UML
		2	NC	UML	NC	UML	NC	UML

(Contd.)

1	*2*	*3*	*4*	*5*	*6*	*7*	*8*	*9*
14.	Udyapur	1	UML	NC	ML	NC	UML	NC
		2	NSP	NC	NC	UML	NC	UML
15.	Saptari	1	UML	NC	NC	UML	NC	UML
		2	NSP	NC	SAD	NC	NC	NSP
		3	NC	NSP	SAD	INDP	RPD	UML
		4	NC	UML	UML	NC	UML	NC
		5	NC	INDP	ML	SAD	NSP	NC
16.	Siraha	1	NC	CPN(D)	NC	UML	UML	NC
		2	NC	INDP	UML	NC	NC	UML
		3	NC	UML	NC	RPP	RPP	NC
		4	INDP	UPF	NC	RPP	UML	NC
		5	UPC	NC	NC	INDP	UML	NC
CDR								
17.	Dolkha	1	UML	NC	NC	UML	UML	NC
		2	UML	NC	ML	NC	UML	NC
18.	Ramechhap	1	NC	UML	UML	NC	UML	NC
		2	UDF	NC	NC	SJMN	NC	SJMN
19.	Sindhuli	1	UML	NC	NC	UML	UML	NC
		2	NC	UML	NC	UML	UML	NC
		3	NC	UDF	NC	RPP	SJMN	NC
20.	Dhanusha	1	NC	UML	UML	NC	NC	UML
		2	NC	UML	NC	UML	UML	NC
		3	NC	UML	NC	UML	NC	RPP
		4	NC	CPN (D)	NC	RPP	RPP	NC
		5	NC	UML	ML	NC	NC	UML
21.	Mahuttari	1	NC	CPN(D)	NC	UML	NC	UML
		2	NC	INDP	RPP(C)	NC	NC	UML
		3	NC	CPN (D)	RPP(T)	NC	NC	RPP
		4	NC	RPP(T)	INDP	NC	NC	RPP
		5	NC	RPP(T)				
22.	Sarlahi	1	NC	UML	UML	NC	UML	NC
		2	NC	NSP	NC	SAD	NSP	RPP

(Contd.)

1	2	3	4	5	6	7	8	9
		3	NC	NSP	NC	SAD	RPP	NC
		4	CPN (D)	RPP(C)	RPP (C)	NC	NC	NSP
		5	NC	INDP	NC	SJMN	NC	RPP
23.	Rasuwa	1	RPP(C)	UML	RPP(C)	NC	NC	UML
24.	Dhading	1	NC	RPP(T)	RPP(T)	NC	RPP	NC
		2	UML	NC	UML	NC	NC	UML
		3	UML	NC	UML	RPP	UML	NC
25.	Nuwakot	1	RPP(T)	UPF	RPP(T)	NC	UML	RPP
		2	UML	RPP(C)	NC	RPP	NC	RPP
		3	NC	UML	NC	RPP	UML	NC
26.	Kathmandu	1	UML	NC	UML	NC	UML	NC
		2	NC	UPF	UML	NC	UML	NC
		3	UML	NC	UML	NC	UML	NC
		4	UML	NC	ML	NC	NC	UML
		5	UML	NC	ML	NC	UML	ML
		6			ML	NC	UML	NC
					UML	NC	NC	UML
27.	Bhaktapur	1	NWPP	NC	MK	RPP	NMKP	NC
		2	NC	NWPP	MK	RPP	NC	NMKP
28.	Lalitpur	1	UML	RPP(T)	UML	NC	UML	Independent
		2	UML	NC	ML	NC	UML	NC
		3	UPF	NC	UML	NC	UML	NC
29.	Kavre	1	UPF	NC	UML	RPP	UML	NC
		2	UML	NC	UML	NC	NC	UML
		3	UML	NC	ML	NC	NC	UML
30.	Sindhupal Chowk	1	UML	NC	UML	RPP	NC	UML
		2	UML	NC	RPP(T)	UML	UML	RPP
		3	RPP(C)	UML	RPP(T)	NC	RPP	UML
31.	Makwanpur	1	UML	RPP(T)	RPP(T)	UML	UML	RPP

(Contd.)

1	*2*	*3*	*4*	*5*	*6*	*7*	*8*	*9*
		2	UML	NC	UML	RPP	UML	RPP
		3	UML	RPP(C)	ML	RPP	UML	RPP
32.	Rauthat	1	NC	CPN(D)	NC	INDP	UML	NC
		2	NC	CPN(D)	NC	INDP	NC	UML
		3	INDP	NC	NC	UML	UML	NC
		4	UML	NC	NC	UML	UML	NC
33.	Bara	1	UML	NC	UML	NC	NC	UML
		2	UML	NC	NC	UML	UML	NC
		3	NC	UML	UML	NC	NC	UML
		4	UML	NC	ML	NC	NC	UML
34.	Parsa	1	NC	UML	RPP(C)	UML	NC	UML
		2	NC	UML	NC	UML	NC	UML
		3	NC	RPP(T)	NC	RPP	NC	UML
		4	NC	UML	NC	UML	UML	NC
35.	Chitwan	1	UML	NC	UML	NC	NC	UML
		2	CPN(D)	NC	UML	NC	NC	UML
		3	UPF	NC	NC	UML	NC	UML
WDR								
36.	Gorkha	1	NC	UPF	NC	RPP	NC	UML
		2	NC	UPF	NC	RPP	NC	UML
		3	NC	UPF	NC	RPP	NC	UML
37.	Manang	1	NC	UPF	NC	UML	NC	UML
38	Lamjung	1	NC	UPF	NC	UML	NC	UML
		2	NC	UML	NC	UML	NC	UML
39.	Kaski	1	NC	UML	UML	NC	NC	UML
		2	UML	NC	UML	NC	NC	UML
		3	UML	NC	NC	UML	NC	UML
40.	Tanahu	1	NC	UPF	NC	UML	NC	UML
		2	NC	UPF	NC	UML	NC	UML
		3	UML	NC	NC	UML	UML	NC
41.	Shyangja	1	NC	UML	ML	NC	UML	NC

(Contd.)

1	*2*	*3*	*4*	*5*	*6*	*7*	*8*	*9*
		2	NC	UML	UNL	NC	NC	UML
		3	NC	UML	ML	NC	NC	UML
		4	NC	UML				
42.	Gulmi	1	NC	UML	UML	NC	UML	NC
		2	NC	UML	UML	NC	UML	NC
		3	NC	UML	ML	NC	UML	NC
43.	Palpa	1	NC	UML	ML	NC	UML	NC
		2	NC	UML	UML	NC	UML	NC
		3	NC	UML	UML	NC	UML	NC
44.	Arghakhanchi	1	NC	UML	NC	UML	RJM	NC
		2	NC	UML	NC	UML	UML	NC
45.	Nawalparasi	1	NC	UML	NC	UML	NC	UML
		2	UML	NC	UML	NC	NSP	NC
		3	NSP	NC	SAD	NC	NSP	NC
		4	NSP	UML	NC	SAD	NC	NSP
46.	Rupandehi	1	NC	UML	NC	UML	NC	RPP(C)
		2	NC	UML	UML	NC	NC	UML
		3	NC	UML	UML	NC	NC	UML
		4	NSP	NC	INDP	SAD	NC	NSP
		5	NSP	NC	RPP(T)	INDP	NSP	RPP
47.	Kapilbastu	1	NC	RPP(T)	NC	UML	UML	NC
		2	NC	RPP(T)	NC	RPP	RPP	NC
		3	NC	NSP	NC	RPP	NC	Independent
		4	NSP	RPP(C)	RPP(T)	NC	RPP	NC
48.	Mustang	1	UML	RPP(C)	NC	RPP	NC	UML
49.	Myangdi	1	UML	NC	UML	RPP	NC	UML
		2	UML	NC				
50.	Baglung	1	NC	UML	LML	NC	NC	UML
		2	NC	RPP(T)	NC	INDP	RJM	NC
		3	INDP	INDP	INDP	INDP	RJM	NC

(Contd.)

1	2	3	4	5	6	7	8	9
51.	Parbat	1	UML	NC	NC	UML	NC	UML
		2	NC	UML	ML	NC	NC	UML
MWDR								
52.	Rukum	1	UPF	NC	NC	UML	NC	UML
		2	NC	UPF	NC	RPP	UML	NC
53.	Rolpa	1	UPF	RPP(T)	RPP(T)	NC	NC	RPP
		2	UPF	NC	NC	UML	NC	UML
54.	Pyuthan	1	NC	UPF	NC	INDP	RJM	ML
		2	NC	UML	INDP	NC	RJM	NC
55.	Salyan	1	NC	UML	NC	UML	UML	NC
		2	NC	UML	NC	RPP	RPP	NC
56.	Dang	1	NC	UML	NC	RPP	NC	RPP
		2	UML	NC	NC	UML	NC	UML
		3	NC	UML	UML	NC	NC	UML
57.	Dolpa	1	NC	RPP(C)	INDP	RPP	UML	Independent
58.	Mugu	1	NC	UML	NC	UML	UML	NC
59.	Jumla	1	NC	UML	MK	INDP	UML	NC
60.	Kalikot	1	NWPP	NC	ML	RPP	UML	NC
61.	Humla	1	UPF	NC	NC	INDP	UML	Independent
62.	Jajarkot	1	NC	RPP(C)	NC	RPP	RPP	UML
		2	UML	NC	NC	UML	UML	Independent
63.	Dailekh	1	NC	NWPP	NC	MKP	UML	NC
		2	NC	NWPP	MK	NC	NC	UML
64.	Surkhet	1	NC	UML	NC	UML	NC	UML
		2	NC	UML	ML	NC	NC	UML
		3			NC	UML	NC	UML
65.	Banke	1	NC	UML	RPP(C)	NC	NC	UML
		2	NC	INDP	RPP(T)	NC	NC	ML
		3	UML	NC	ML	NC	NC	UML

(Contd.)

1	*2*	*3*	*4*	*5*	*6*	*7*	*8*	*9*
FWDR								
66.	Bajura	1	NC	UML	ML	NC	NC	UML
67.	Achham	1	NC	UML	UML	NC	NC	RPP(C)
		2	NC	UML	ML	NC	NC	UML
		3	NC	RPP(T)				
68.	Bajhang	1	NC	UML	UML	NC	NC	UML
		2	NC	UML	IWDP	UML	NC	UML
69.	Doti	1	NC	RPP(C)	NC	UML	NC	UML
		2	NC	RPP(C)	NC	RPP	NC	RPP(C)
70.	Kailali	1	NC	RPP(T)	UML	NC	NC	UML
		2	NC	UML	NC	RPP	NC	RPP
		3	NC	UML	UML	NC	NC	UML
71.	Darchula	1	NC	CPN (D)	ML	RPP	NC	UML
		2	RPP(T)	NC	UML	NC		
Baitadi								
		1	NC	RPP (C)	RPP(C)	UML	NC	UML
		2	NC	CPN(D)	RPP(C)	NC	NC	UML
		3	NC	RPP(C)				
	Dadeldhura	1	NC	UML	NC	JBMN	NC	UML
72.	Kanchanpur	1	NC	UML	UML	NC	NC	UML
		2	NC	UML	ML	NC	NC	UML
		3					NC	RPP(C)

Source: Documents of the Election Commission, HMG, Nepal.

Concluding Observations

A constitution and periodical elections are considered to be the core of democracy in a country. While the first provides a framework of governance the structures, rolls and norms and procedures of works, rights and duties, the other provides dynamism to the functioning of democracy. These are indeed essential prerequisites and also ensure the availability of the other core aspects of the working of democracy.

Taking these aspects into consideration, one may safely argue that Nepal has a viable structural foundation of democracy in the post-1990 period. Nepal's 1990 constitution does provide for a structure of democratic government in the country. It is a different issue that the constitution has not been framed by a body of people's representatives. It is true that a democratic constitution should have been framed by a Constituent Assembly constituted by the representatives of the people. But if the spirit of democracy is there a constitution framed by a constitution making committee can be acceptable. The more important point here is how the provisions of the constitution are implemented and followed. It is equally important to what extent the political elite has faith on constitutionalism and democracy. That the constitutional provisions are not made an instrument for the realization of personal political ambitions. It much depends on the perception of the political elite. If they have a democratic perception and faith on democratic governance, respect to the provisions of the constitution will be followed. If the perception is authoritarian and individualistic than violation of the constitution may take place. So Nepal's problem has not been that of the framework of the constitution, so much so, the perception and individualistic political ambitions of the political elite—more specifically the traditional political elite. So the issue pertinent here is not that of the theoretical postulates of constitution but the perception of the political elite prevailing in the implementation of the constitution. The point is that it was the individual perception and political ambitions of king Gyanendra which altered the course of democracy in Nepal by using constitutional provisions for his own use.

The three general elections have provided dynamism to democracy in Nepal. This dynamism stopped as the democratic process was thwarted after 2002 after the personal perception prevailed over popular perception. It may, however, be pointed here that the general elections have so far failed in laying down the foundation of a strong majoritarian governance in Nepal. This could be due to three reasons. After a long gap of 30 years the popular participation in the electoral process could not gain dynamism. The political parties have not been able to enjoy wide social base. Lastly, due to the negative performance of the political parties on many counts popular participation has been rather discouraged.

To sum up the discussion it needs to be remembered that the theoretical postulates of the structures of democracy are by itself not important. The political actors are equally important who actually give dynamism to the various provisions of the constitution.

REFERENCES

1. See for further discussions: P. Samuel H. Barnes *et al., Political Action, Mass participation in Five Western Democracies,* Beverly Hill, London, 1979. Juan Linz, *et al.,* Problems of Democratic Transition and Consolidation, Baltimore, 1996.
2. *The Patriot* (New Delhi), March 1, 1991.
3. These were Communist Party of Nepal (Amatya), Communist Party of Nepal (Verma), Communist Party of Nepal (Fourth Convention and Nepal Labourers and Peasants Organisation).
4. *The CPN* (Manandhar) group was also involved in the formation of the UML but it later decided to retain its independent identity.
5. *The Times of India* (New Delhi), May 12, 1990.
6. *The Times of India* (New Delhi), May 12, 1990.
7. *The Times of India* (New Delhi), May 12, 1990.
8. *Gorkhapatra,* (Nepali daily Kathmandu), May 13, 1990 (Nepal Press Digest), vol. 34, No. 21, May 21, 1990.
9. *Gorkhapatra,* (Kathmandu), May 16, 1990.
10. *Pristhabhumi,* (Weekly, Kathmandu), May 24, 1990.
11. N. 10.
12. *Gorkhapatra,* (Kathmandu), May 30, 1990.
13. *Saptahik Nepali Awaz* (Kathmandu), June 1, 1990.
14. *The Rising Nepal* (Kathmandu), May 30, 1990.
15. See, Text of the Constitution of the kingdom of Nepal 2047 (1990) HMG, Kathmandu November, 1990.
16. N. 15.
17. N. 15.
18. Samuel P. Huntington and M. Naison, *No Easy Choice, Political Participation in Developing Countries,* Harward University Press, 1967: 4.
19. Ira Sharkansky, *The Policy Predicament,* Making and Implementing Public Policy, W.H. Freeman & Company, San Francisco, 1978: 21-23.
20. Leslie Lipson, *The Democratic Civilization,* Oxford University Press, New York, 1964: 274.
21. *The Economic Times,* November 13, 1990.
22. *Spotlight* (Kathmandu), May 31, 1990: 9.

23. B.C. Upreti, *The Nepali Congress, An Analysis of the Party's Performance in the General Elections and its Aftermath*, Nirala Publications, New Delhi, 1993: 98.
24. *Nepali Patra*, (Kathmandu), March 15, 1991.
25. *Gorkhapatra*, March 26, 1991.
26. *Gorkhapatra*, April 4, 1991.
27. *Gorkhapatra*, April 3, 1991.
28. *Gorkhapatra*, April 5, 1991.
29. B.C. Upreti, N. 23: 61-62.
30. R.C. Mathur, "India Factor to the Fore in Nepal". *The Hindustan Times*, May 12, 1996. D.P. Kumar, S.D. Mani, "India Factor in Nepal's Election" *The Times of India*, May 6, 1991.
31. B.C. Upreti, N. 23 : 90-116.
32. *Rasthra Pukar* (Kathmandu), July 13, 1994.
33. *Kantipur* (Nepali Daily), July 15, 1994.
34. *The Nepal Post*, July 15, 1994.
35. *The Rising Nepal*, October 6, 1994; *Gorkhapatra*, October 6, 1994 .
36. *Gorkhapatra*, October 6, 1994, October 18, 1994.
37. *The Rising Nepal*, October 25, 1994.
38. *Gorkhapatra*, October 11, 1994.
39. Data provided by the Election Commission, HMG, Kathmandu; 1999 Election handouts.

5

Social Discontents and Democracy

The Social context in which a democratic system is operating plays a significant role in its success or failure. Democracy is a term that can be used in a similar way as 'freedom' or 'equality' is used.[1] The way we talk of freedom to all or equality to all, we can also talk of democracy to all. When democracy does not relate to all and it remains confined to a few in the society, say a majoritarian group, it generates problems in the society. It divides the people into majoritarian and minority groups. The majoritarian group becomes a privileged one while the minorities are deprived of their rights. It leads to a conflicting situation in the society thereby generating social tensions and diffusion, weakening the state and disrupting the democratic order. It is for this reason that the social context of democracy becomes important in the plural societies.[2] It is a fact that social inequalities inherited from the past or created, that confer political advantages for some people and groups and corresponding disadvantages for others create problems and challenges to social cohesion and integrity.

In plural societies the task of democratic governance is to eradicate the traditional social hierarchies that have been the root cause of inequalities. As the democracy works, the constraint of social stratification produces protests against inequalities.[3] One has to be reminded here that a democratic system is an expression of the principle of political equality. The social inequality contradicts the principle of political equality. Therefore, political equality can be possible only when there is social equality in the society.

Many theorists on democracy talked of popular participation in a democratic system.[4] It is true that direct participation of people in politics is an essential feature of democracy. But that itself does not ensure social equality. The point is that the elected government can not have a monopoly over power. The political process does not began and end with elections, which is one opportunity of popular participation in politics. The democratic governance has to create conditions for social equality and parity. The democracy needs to create strong foundation of shared values and shared experiences.[5] This process would attain social equality. The success of a democratic system and its sustainability depends on to what extent it has been able to create conditions for social equality.

The plural societies are complex societies. The society is divided between various large or small groups on the basis of ethnicity, caste, religion, etc. While all these groups aspire for freedom, rights and equality, it is not possible due to majoritarian control over power and resources. It causes discontent among the minority groups. Their discontent may remain latent so long there is a feudal and authoritarian system. But with the dawn of democracy these latent forces begun to mobilize and a conflicting situation arises. It is the responsibility of the democratic governance to resolve these discontents and establish equality. Thus democracy opens opportunity for the exposition of social discontent and democracy alone can provide answer to it.

Social inequalities may occur due to two reasons:

1. Social inequalities and discrimination inherited from the past traditions, where a feudal authoritarian system gives rise to a hierarchical social order. The inequalities are inherent in a hierarchical social order.
2. Social inequalities and discriminations created due to the authoritarian nature of the political order and faculty policies of modernization and development.

In fact, how a society evolves and in what manner the rulers allow it to grow are important factors in this regard. The social discriminations and inequalities have wider political and economic ramifications. The authoritarian ruling elite have a vested interest in the perpetuation of the hierarchical and discriminatory social order. As and when this authoritarian order is replaced by a democratic political order the discontent against discrimination and inequalities also starts to surfacing. Therefore, democracy in a plural society is bound to face challenges from the society so long as the political order and the social order remain contradictory to each other.

Nature of Nepalese Society

The present day social discontent in Nepal has its roots in the traditional state and society of Nepal. It is, therefore, relevant here to understand the evolution and nature of Nepalese society.

The modern state of Nepal came into existence in 1769. Before this, Nepal was divided into several small principalities. There were 46 small states in the east and west of Kathmandu valley known as *Baise* and *Chaubisi* states, representing different ethno-religious groups and communities that were rival to each other. These apart there were tribal states of Kosi and Gandaki basins; Newar rulers of Kathmandu valley and the Sen of Palpa. Prithvinarayan Shah a ruler of the Gurkha principality took up a military adventure and invaded and defeated various principalities and the rulers of Nepal. He then founded the kingdom of Nepal in 1769. King Prithvinaryan Shah was conscious of the fact that the kingdom of Nepal was founded by the forced unification of diverse ethno-cultural groups that were inimical to and fighting with each other for their existence. It was indeed a matter of great consideration that these principalities had been brought together through a military expedition. It was not possible to sustain a kingdom on the basis of military power alone on a long-term basis. There was a need to evolve a socio-cultural milieu that would give shape to a monolithic social order in Nepal. There was also a need to evolve a strong socio-religious base to king's rule.

King Prithvinarayan Shah tried to define state in religio-cultural terms.[6] It was declared by the king that all the land resources of Nepal would automatically fall under his possession and control. The land was identified as *Desa* (the country) and the people as realm. King was projected as the sovereign lord, and the king had proprietary authority over both. The king was accorded a religious basis and was declared as the representative of Lord Vishnu and that way he got the right to rule the Des and realm both. Thus, the king was projected as a sovereign over the land; a protector of his subjects and territory and source of all aspirations, rules and traditions. King Prithvinarayan Shah adopted a multi-dimensional approach in order to build a strong and unified Nepali society and state. He followed a stratified hierarchical model for the society based on the *Chaturvarna* Hindu caste system. The Brahmins and the Kshatriyas (Rajputs) were accorded top place in this hierarchical order. They were called *Tagadharis* who had the authority to wear the sacred thread and perform all kind of religious rituals. Next in the hierarchy were the *Matwalis*. The *Matwalis* were further divided into two categories; unsalvageable *Matwalis* and salvageable *Matwalis*. All the ethnic groups were classified under these categories. On the whole there were four *varnas* and *chattis jats* (thirty-six castes). Jang Bahadur Rana further classified them in his *Mulki Ain* of 1854.[7]

The social set-up thus evolved had Brahminic supremacy. As a result the Brahmins acquired social prestige and also gained supremacy in politico-economic and administrative fields. The Kshatriyas (Thakuris) had next place in the social hierarchy. They got positions in the royal palace. They were the protector of royal authority. As a result they enjoyed power, privileges by the king and hold over land.

What is important here is that in the hierarchical social order of Nepal, it was the Brahminis and Kshatriyas of the hill region who were accorded positions of power and privileges. This bowed seeds of regional disparities as well. Because it was the Brahmins and Kshatriyas of the hill region who became repository of the hill culture and acquired significance in the power structure. Henceforth, identification with the hill culture and caste hierarchy became important in determining power and prestige of social groups.[8] The people of Tarai were encouraged to follow the hill cultural traits,[9] which they resented and consequently they got dissatisfied and felt being discriminated.

The Shah rulers started a process of Hinduaization in order to form a monolithic society. The non-Hindu tribal communities were motivated as well as forced, to accept the Hindus religion. They were categorized under the Hindu hierarchical caste order. All tribal people were placed in the lowest web of the social order. A policy of compensation and accommodation was also followed in order to bring non-Hindu communities within the fold of Hinduism. The Magars were allowed to wear scared thread as recognition to the services that they had rendered to the Palace. King Prithvinarayan Shah said, "I am the king of Magrant." It was indeed an emotional attempt to assimilate Magars. The Gurungs were also rewarded for the services rendered by them to the Gurkha rulers. Autonomy was also given to Limbus for sometime.

The Shah Rulers though recognized plurality, did not accord rights and status to different ethnic groups and communities. The monarchy accorded protection to Hindu temples and shrines. Crime was graded on the basis of caste and punishment was fixed accordingly. The Brahmins were excluded from capital punishment. Thus, Brahminic supremacy became hallmark of Nepali state and society.

A unified religious and cultural policy was persuaded. Nepal was given the status of a Hindu state. King Prithvinarayan Shah said 'Yo Asli Hindustan Hao' (This is the real Hindustan). The *Gorkhali* or the *Khas Kura* was designated as the language of Nepal in the form of Nepali.

The Shah and the Rana rulers adopted policy of consolidation of the tribal areas. Once the tribal rulers were defeated Brahmins and Chettris were sent in these areas to take up the local administration in their hands. Land was confiscated from the tribal landlords under the *kipat* land system and it was redistributed to Brahmins and Kshatriyas under *Raikar, Birta, Guthi* and *Jagir* system. New settlement of the high caste people in tribal areas was encouraged. A large number of high caste Brahmins and Kshatriyas became absentee landlords in these areas. High caste people were also encouraged to migrate to these areas. Thus, the indigenous people were exploited under the new system. The policy of patrimonialism, rewards and punishment continued. Thus a patrimonial state and society emerged in Nepal. The hierarchical relations became dominating in the society.

It is clear that the Nepali rulers followed a policy of forced cultural unification of different ethnic groups. Efforts were made to bring various tribal groups, belonging to the Mongoloid racial stock, under the fold of Hinduism. Hinduism served dual objectives of social and political order.[10] The institution of monarchy was a rallying point between the high caste Hindus of the hills and the other ethnic groups. It may also be pointed out here that the Nepali rulers deliberately kept various communities isolated and underdeveloped. Actually, the ruling elite wanted to lay down a foundation of a unified model under the framework of Hinduism.

Obviously, no efforts could be made towards the socio-economic upliftment of backward communities, assuming that it would generate consciousness among them, ultimately being detrimental to the authoritarian rule of the monarchy and the Ranas. The state that thus emerged in Nepal was a predatory Hindu state.[11]

The social order that emerged historically was protected in the post-1950 period. The monarchy tried to assert upon political authority on the basis of the Hindu identity of the state and the society. After 1960 when King Mahendra gave an alternative model to the country in the form of panchayat system he defended it on the basis of the traditional socio-political order of Nepal.[12] Monarchy always used the sword of Hinduism in order to establish its political prominence. The Hindu state survived in Nepal. And the Hindu identity of state perpetuated. Thus, in Nepal society, state and the institution of monarchy evolved with strong interlink ages. It was naturally based on social and political discriminations. The post-1950 political elite continued to depend on such a social order because of its strong identification with the state.

Emerging Issues and Problems of Social Inequalities and Discontent

It was obvious that the way Nepali society evolved it will give rise to social discontents and tensions. This discontent has become prominent in the post-1990 period with the down of democracy in the country. There are three major streams of societal discontent and movements in Nepal, which are being discussed here. Our basic purpose here is to underline the fact that the emerging social discontent in Nepal has posed a challenge to democracy.

THE DALIT MOVEMENT

The socio-religious differentiation is an essential feature of the caste oriented traditional societies. In such societies two distinct groups of people are clearly visible. The upper strata–consisting of ruling class and privileged groups of people and the lower strata–consisting of people of oppressed and disadvantaged categories. It is expected transformation of these societies to modernization, development and democracy will lead to the upward mobility of the depressed sections of the society. Constitutionally all people are considered equal and a democratic constitution envisages for social equality, freedom and rights. But it has been observed that due to deep rooted traditions, customs and majoritarian hold over power there exits inequality and discrimination among various strata of the society. In a multi-cultural society such problems are wide spread, and the problem of their upliftment often becomes a challenge for the society and polity.

The dalits form the lowest web of the society in the social hierarchy. They form the oppressed, suppressed and disadvantaged groups of the society. The dalits have also been termed as untouchables. Because of their lower position in the society they have been subject to all kinds of exploitations and intimidations by the upper class people.[13]

In the Nepali social structure there are two categories of people: (1) the people of caste origin, (2) the people of non-caste origin. In the first group there are four caste categories. The dalits or untouchables form the lowest category in the caste category (Matwali-uncleans).[14]

Socio-Economic Conditions of Dalits

It is estimated that 15 per cent of the total population of Nepal comes under the category of dalits. The dalits are scattered all over the country. The dalits are characterized by illiteracy, poverty, menial jobs, marginal living conditions and social abuses and ill-treatment.[15] The dalits are generally subject to four types of discriminations.

1. Social discriminations—lowest category in the caste hierarchy treated in the society as untouchables.
2. Religious discrimination—not allowed interring religious places and performing puja (worship).
3. Occupational discrimination—allowed performing menial jobs only that are prohibited for the upper caste people.
4. Territorial discrimination—the dalits were allowed to live in the fringe areas of the urban or rural localities with minimum or no facilities.

As a result of these differentiations dalits had no access to resources and they were marginalized in the social and political life of the country.[16]

It is true that after 1950 certain legal measures were being taken up for the emancipation of dalits but due to strong socio-religious traditions, feudalistic nature of the society and for political reasons they remained theoretical notions than having any practical worth. The *Mulki Ain* of 2020 called for emancipation of dalits. Legal prohibitions were laid on caste discriminations. But nothing much happened to the deprived lot of dalits. Despite an increasing awareness in many parts of the hill areas the position of untouchability has been widely in use. The dalits are not supposed to touch water, milk, food, etc. They cannot take food along with the people of upper castes. They cannot fetch drinking water from the same water place that is being used by the Savarnas. In fact, these became social norms and practices in the traditional society of Nepal. The practice of purification has been still in use (*Choi Chito halno parne*). The people getting married with dalits are socially punished.

Dalit Awakening and Unity

The dalits of Nepal are also gradually awakening and realizing about their pitiable socio-economic conditions. The social change coming up in Nepal has also touched the dalits. The educated people among dalits are feeling that they are being discriminated. Awareness is growing among dalits and they are trying to organize themselves. The question of empowerment of dalits is being taken up at different forums. In Kathmandu and other places the question of dalits and ways and means for their emancipation and upliftment are being discussed in various academic forums.[17] Dalits are now associating with different political parties in order to seek their support. A large number of dalit organizations have come up in Nepal during last few years.[18] Some of them are:

	Organisation	*Year of Formation in VS*
1.	Vishwa Sarwajan Sangh	2004
2.	Tailor Union	2004
3.	Nepal Samaj Sudhar Sangh	2004
4.	Nepal Harijan Sangh	2007
5.	Jate Tod Mandal	2008
6.	Samaj Sudhar Sangh	2009
7.	Parigarit Neri Sangh	2012
8.	Nepal Rashtriya Parigabit Parishad	2014
9.	Acht Mukti Morcha	2015
10.	Rashtriya Achut Mukti Parishad	2015

(Contd.)

	Organisation	*Year of Formation in VS*
11.	Nepal Rashtriya Jan Vikas Parishad	2024
12.	Samaj Sudhar Sangh	2036
13.	Pachaute Jati Sudhar Sangh	2037
14.	Nepal Ati Pichadiyae ka Jan Vikas Parishad	2038
15.	Nepal Rashtriya Samaj Kalyan Sangh	2039
16.	Chuachut Kukti Sangthan	2040
17.	Jatiya Wiwad Unmulan Manch	2044
18.	Utpidit Jatiya Utthan Manch	2045
19.	Nepal Rashtriya Dalit Mukti Morcha	2046
20.	Utpidit Janjatiya Mukti Morcha	2046
21.	Vikasonmukh Samaj Sangh	2048
22.	Nepal Dalit Utthan Sangh	2048
23.	Nepal Utpidit Dalit Jatiya Mukti Samaj	2049
24.	Rashtriya Prajatantrik Utpidit Jan Utthan Sangthan	2049
25.	Nepal Dalit Shramik Morcha	2053
26.	Utpidit Jatiya Chetana Sangh	2053
27.	Nepal Dalit Sangh	2054
28.	Nepal Utpidit Jatiya Mukti Samaj	2055
29.	Nepal Dalit Mukti Morcha	2055
30.	Prajatantrik Dalit Sangthan	2055
31.	Nepal Dalit Utthan Manch	2057
32.	Dalit Gau-Sarkari Sanstha Mahasangh	2054

The formation of these organizations indicates that there is an increased awareness among dalits and they are trying to assert in an increased organized way for the realization of their demands. It is also clear that in comparison to the earlier years more organizations have come up after the establishment of democracy in the country.

Dalit Demands and Strategies

The dalit organizations have generally concentrated upon the following demands:

1. The dalits are becoming conscious of their marginalized position; therefore, they demand that an action oriented plan be prepared for the upliftment of dalits.

2. Strong steps taken against social discrimination to dalits. All kinds of social prejudices, atrocities and exploitation of dalits should be strictly prohibited.
3. Discrimination at the religious places should be banned.
4. Separate identity of dalits needs to be preserved by inacting a legislation in this regard.
5. Special drives to impart education to dalits.
6. Special funds be provided for the development of dalit localities.
7. The government has to ensure that dalits get adequate representation in civil services and other governmental institutions, political institutions, educational institutions and so on.
8. Introduction of land reforms measures so that dalits get share in land in proportion to their strength.

Problems and Issues

It is not sufficient to make constitutional and other legal provisions for the upliftment of dalits. In caste oriented traditional societies there exists a strong foundation of social hierarchies and social divisions. It is not possible to remove them merely by enacting a law against it. It needs a change in the preparation, attitude or behaviour of society towards the dalits. It requires social transformation and social change. One has to learn that it is not possible to transform any society overnight. It is a gradual and long-term process. Any body's consideration would be to observe whether a society is moving on to that direction firmly. What is required here is a clear legislations and changing perception of the people in accordance to the implementation of these legislations. Nepal's problem is that there have been a strong hierarchical order and feudalistic orientation of the society. This feudalistic nature of the society perpetuated and further strengthened by the authoritarian nature of the state. The Brahmin–Chettri–Newar caste groups dominated the higher echelons of Nepali society, economy and polity. The ruling elite were highly dependent on these caste groups. So, the ruling elite adopted a status quoist approach, despite some headway towards the emancipation of dalits through some legalistic measures. Even after 1990 there does not appear to be much change in terms of social transformation, perceptional change, etc. Though there are constitutional measures, increased consciousness among the dalits and an increase in their organizational support bases.

There are some other specific issues and problems, which can be highlighted here:

(i) The socio-economic conditions of the dalits are still very miserable. The illiteracy, poverty, backwardness and menial job orientation is rampant among them. Unless a change occurs in this situation it is difficult for them to prepare themselves for a long-term fight for rights, freedom and equality.

(ii) Dalits are not a socially cohesive group. Even among the dalits there is hierarchy and that divides them.

(iii) Politically as well, the dalits are divided. There are dalit organizations associated with Nepali Congress, UML, Sadbhavana Party and so on.[19] All the political parties have vested interests in associating dalit organizations with them. A united dalit movement will be a rare possibility so long the dalits remain divided, politically.

The dalit issue is important in the Nepali context. It is essential to resolve this problem in order to build a cohesive and integrated society, which indeed forms a hallmark of a successful democracy. There is an increased consciousness regarding the dalit question. But reservation to dalit is still a controversial issue. The 1990 constitution did not say anything in this regard and it is difficult to say anything definitely whether it would be included in the forthcoming constitutional exercise. Nevertheless, one would like to say that the dalit issue has become important and it is likely to remain at the forefront of politics of Nepal in coming years. There are more possibilities of the politicization of the dalit question in future.

ETHNIC ISSUES AND PROBLEMS

In plural–societies mobilization of individuals and groups on the basis of ethnicity is an important feature. When various smaller groups and communities realize that they are being discriminated by the majority communities that also form the ruling elite, they begun to assert for their rights on the basis of their traditional identity. It leads to the ethnicisation of politics and the politicization of ethnicity.

Ethnicity has been a source of tensions and conflicts in many societies; to the extent that the ethnic movements have given rise to separatist tendencies resulting into disintegration of state. So, it is a fact that in plural societies social solidarity and stability can be maintained only by ensuring a balance between different ethnic groups in terms of distribution of resources and benefits.

In Nepal ethnicity is gradually becoming an important variable in the politics. In fact, the issues such as the formation of various organizations on ethnic lines, demand for regional and ethnic autonomy, political tensions arising due to unequal distribution of power among various communities and regions, etc., are becoming critical factors of Nepali politics. The long-standing domination of the Brahmin–Chettri–Newar trio has come under severe criticism by ethnic groups. The Hindu Tribal communities, which are undergoing fast social and political mobilization are challenging the traditional power base of the Nepali society and polity and also trying to assert for equitable redistribution of resources and goods.

In fact, it can be said that as the political and economic structures of the country have become competitive and ethnic mobilization is taking place, various underprivileged ethnic groups have started demanding a greater share in societal and services.

Ethnic Groups and Communities

A brief look at the various ethnic groups will help us in understanding the plural nature of Nepali society. Nepal has a multi-racial, multi-lingual and multi-cultural society. Its inhabitants can be classified into three main racial stocks: The Indo-Aryans, the Mongoloids and the Austro-Asiatic. Majority of the population of the country is Hindus followed by Buddhists, Muslims and Christians.[20]

The people speaking various languages and dialects of the Indian origin who had migrated from India to Nepal at different points of time are Indo-Aryans. They became part and parcel of Nepali society in due course. They are settled in both the hill areas and the Tarai region of the kingdom. In the Tarai region a large number of people of the Indian origin migrated at a later stage are still awaited citizenship of Nepal. The people of Mongoloid origin such as Rai, Limbu, Tamang, Sunwar, Gurung, Magar, Kirati, Bhote, Sherpa, Chepang, Thakali, etc., are settled in the Himalayan and the hill regions. They are believed to have migrated to Nepal from the north. Their language, culture and life-style are quite similar to those of the people of Tibet. The people of Austro-Asiatic origin are Sutar, Dura, Dunwar, Rawate, Santhali, etc.

The people of the Tarai region that is constituted of the Indian migrants and the tribal groups have a regional identity. They include plains Brahmin, Rajputs, Banias, Bhumihar, Yadav, Kayastha, Kurmi, Rauyniyar and the tribals like, Tharu, Sutar Rajbansis Dhina, Jhangad, etc. There are dalit groups in the hills and Tarai. The Newar mostly dwelling the Kathmandu valley have a separate cultural identity. There are Muslims and Christians as well. Muslims mostly dwell the Tarai region.

Patterns of Ethnic Mobilization and Demand Politics

There were indications of resurgence of pan-tribal sentiments in Nepal towards the end of the seventies. The people of Mongolian origin had strong feelings against discrimination towards them. In September 1979, K.B. Gurung convened a conference of the people of Mongoloid origin. The conference demanded proportionate representation of the Mongoloids in the public sector. Gurung questioned the validity of declaring Nepal a Hindu state and demanded that Nepal should be declared a secular state.[21]

The 1979 movement for democracy and the consequent referendum of 1980 did evoke tribal sentiments but it seems that the Mongoloid people failed in mobilizing themselves on ethnic lines in an organized manner largely due to systemic prohibitions.

Various ethnic identities again started surfacing in the political arena of Nepal after the establishment of democracy in the country in 1990. It has given a new dimension of ethno-politics in the country. It may be noted here that in three years time after 1990, nearly 44 ethnic associations had come to existence by the end of 1993.[22] It clearly reflects upon the mobilization of ethnic groups after the dawn democracy in the country.

The resurgence of Mongoloid ethic groups took a new turn after 1990. With the beginning of the democratic process a number of tribal ethnic identities have surfaced. These organizations began to assert for the promotion of their interests. On the eve of the 1991 general elections Nepal Rashtriya Jana Jati Party demanded division of Nepal into 12 autonomous regions such as *Khasan, Jadan, Magarat, Tamuan, Tamba Saling, Nepal, Khmbuan, Limbuan, Kohila,* Maithili, *Bhojpuri* and *Awadhi.*[23] Thus, demands for regional autonomy on ethno-linguistic lines began to surface. The issue of language also got complicated with the use of language other than Nepali in the parliament.

Following the use of Hindi language in the Nepali Parliament by the members of the Sadbhavana Party, the parliamentarians of the hill ethnic groups also began to speak in their own languages. The ethnic groups are highly critical of Brahminic hold of politics.[24] The strong reactions of the ethnic Mongloids against undermining their religio-cultural identity and their underprivileged position against the Brahmin–Chettri–Newar domination have reflected in the expressions of the Mongoloid leaders. Bir Nembang a Mongal leader raised voice for a separate self-ruled state in Limbuwan while Hark Raj Limbu formed a 'Limbuwan National Council. Rais on the other hand have demanded for a separate Khambuan.[25]

Ethnic groups have also expressed strong reactions against the discriminatory traditions of the Nepali society, by violating certain norms such as *Pani Ubau Andolan* (touch water movement) by untouchable castes and resentment against *Pani na calne-choi chito halnu naparne* and *Pani* na *clane choi chito halno parne* traditions. Some tribal groups have started publishing news papers and other literature in their languages. The literature in indigenous languages is being provided to them free of cost. The educated people of the ethnic groups are providing leadership in this regard. A neo-rich class has also emerged among Mongoloid in the course of time, which is also providing leadership and resources. A number of teachers in the university and colleges belonging to a particular ethnic group are providing leadership to it.

In nutshell the Mongolian ethnic groups have following major problems.

1. Cultural hegemony of the Hindus.
2. Nepal's continuation as a Hindu State.
3. Perpetuation of *Bahunvad* (Brahminism) and domination of Brahmins and Chettris in the political and administrative structures of the country.
4. Inadequate political representation of the ethnic communities.
5. Faulty Census procedures that reduces their numerical strength.
6. Question of distinct cultural identity.

7. Social and economic inequalities and discrimination.
8. Economic backwardness of ethnic groups. The development policies have failed to change quality of life of the people of Mongolian origin.

Since the formation of political parties on religious and cultural basis is prohibited in the constitution of 1990, the various ethnic groups sought alignment with one or the other political parties. The later have tried to exploit the organized strength of these ethnic groups for their own purposes and have tried to patronage the ethnic leadership. In fact, the ethnic leadership is seeking support from their own ethnic organizations as well as the political party to which they have sought affiliation. However, political parties still do not appear to be too much concerned to ethnic demands, particularly due to the prevailing structures of political parties, which go largely in favour of Brahmin–Chettri cliques. The Maoists seem to be more concerned to ethnic demands. Some of the demands of ethnic groups and the Maoists are similar. Therefore, there has been a convergence of interest of the two. It was for this reason as well, that the young people of some of the Mongolian communities joined the Maoist movement. If the ethnic groups are politicized further it may pose new challenge to Nepali state.[26]

Problem of Regionalism

The people of Tarai region have been discriminated in Nepal historically. The hill people and the ruling elite did not trust them ever. Hence, they had strong resentments against the state. After 1950 people of the Tarai region began to assert against the domination of the hill people. The major discontent of the Madhesias was against their under representation in the political structures, bureaucracy and army. During the fifties the people of Tarai also tried to assert their linguistic identity and demanded status and recognition to Hindi, which was a lingua–Franca among all the communities of the Tarai. A 'Save Hindi Movement' was launched in the Tarai during the fifties. But not only that the discrimination against people of Tarai continued the citizenship rules were framed in a way to make it difficult for them to obtain Nepali citizenship.

After the introduction of the panchayat system in 1962, deliberate attempts were made to encourage Nepali language in the Tarai in place of Hindi, migration of hill people in the Tarai and the consolidation of citizenship rules. The people of the hill region migrating to Tarai were given surplus land by introducing land reforms. The surplus land was denied to the Tarai people who had been the tiller of the land for a long time. The people of the Tarai region viewed these steps as a deliberate denial of rights to them and a cultural invasion over them by the hill people. The *Madhesias* were considered as a second rate citizens. However, since organized political activities had been banned under the Panchayat System, the discontent among the people of the Tarai region remained more or less latent.[27] The resentment of the people of the Tarai region has surfaced in a big way in the post-1990 Nepali politics. The Nepal Sadbhavana Party has come forward to protect the interest of the people of Tarai. It aims at fighting against the discrimination towards the Tarai people and the policies of 'Nasalization' vis-a-vis Madhesias.[28]

It clearly indicates that the Tarai people are not only unhappy with their disproportionate representation in the power structure but also with the hill cultural hegemony. During the May 1991 general elections Sadbhavana Party raised ethnic issues and demanded regional autonomy for the Tarai, declaration of Hindi as an official language of Nepal, citizenship to all the people of Tarai and 50 per cent reservations for the people of Tarai in army and administration.

It can be said here that the ethnic issues are coming up in Nepal in recent years. It has both cultural and regional dimensions. State has been held responsible for the rise of ethnic and regional issues and the Hindu identity of state has been the cause of concern particularly among the non-Hindu groups.

It is clear that the restructuring of state is becoming a major issue in Nepali politics. The Hindu identity of state might not prove to be strong enough to deal with the emerging challenges. There is an urge in Nepal to change the national identity. The ethnic groups and the Maoists are demanding for a secular state. The Madhesis, dalits and other marginalized communities also support the cause of secular identity and liberal values. Therefore, the emerging trends of ethnicity call for restructuring of state and the accommodation of diverse groups within a liberal democratic socio-political order. It is only through this approach that the project of nation building can be pushed up in Nepal in the changing context.

MAOIST INSURGENCY

Maoists as a social group has a broader framework that include dalits as well as the ethnic groups, along with other sections of the society. Maoists have raised many of those issues for which the dalits and the ethnic groups have been trying to mobilize themselves in an organized manner. However, the Maoist movement can be looked upon as a broader socio-political movement. It would not be wrong to say that the Maoists in a way represented the growing discontent in the Nepalese society. The way Maoists gained popularity in the countryside and expanded their influence and control over a large part of the country sufficiently speaks of the support it received from the various sections of the society.[29] It is a different issue that the Maoist movement took a violent turn for political reasons and consequently lost much of the sympathy of the masses.

Our purpose here is to look at the Maoist movement from a sociological perspective and dwell upon social concerns and implications of the Maoist movement. The Maoists formed of those ultra leftists communists who despite their much dissatisfaction joined the democratic process after 1990 but were frustrated soon. They realized that it was not possible for them to assert upon power through constitutional means. Hence, they took a revolutionary path. It is difficult to place Maoists in a clear theoretical perspective. It was a group influenced by and using the restructuring ideology of Mao to Shining path. It believed in socio-economic transformation but thought that it was possible by getting hold of political powers. In terms of caste-class analysis, like any other political group, its leadership belonged to the upper strata of the society. But its supporters were drawn from all sections of the society. Their strategy was to capture the rural areas through guerilla war.

The Maoists have believed in the establishment of a new democratic order in the country, which they called 'people's government'. The people's government was supposed to work for the elimination of social and economic hierarchies and discriminations. The focal point of their concern was the feudal structure of the Nepalese society and the exploitative and absolutist nature of the political system. They believed that the emancipation of the Nepalese people from the prevailing conditions was possible only through a war, which they term as 'people's war'. Explaining the people's war a Maoist leader said:

> "People's war' is a war waged by the oppressed people against their oppressors for liberation. The oppressor class has always been oppressing the majority through violence ever since class and the state power originated in the world. The oppressed class, therefore, is forced to resort counter–violence in order to create and maintain a new state power by pulling down the old one for the sake of its liberation. The people's war is a struggle of counter violence waged by the people against the oppressor class and its state power. The people's war assumes a long-term character in any society in which the small property owners or peasants are in the majority. There is disparity in the pace of progress in different parts of the country, and the revolutionary class has to struggle against a powerful enemy force."[30]

The Maoists strongly opposed the view that it was a struggle of a terrorist or extremist nature. Instead their contention was that it was a class–struggle waged by the communist revolutionaries and based on the class-character of the Nepalese society.[31] Further explaining the ideology and the objectives of the Maoists struggle Babu Ram Bhattarai, one of the top leaders of Maoists had said:

> "We want to overthrow the present state and establish a new democratic republic which will be neither communist nor socialist. In our new democratic republic, there will be no place for feudal, comprador, bureaucratic and capitalist forces, which are now flourishing under the protection and influence of foreign imperialist powers. We want to form a joint government of patriotic and democratic forces. The new system need not be a one party system, but can also be a multi-party system."[32]

The Maoist romanticism of establishing a classless society free of exploitation attracted a large number of people to join their army. The educated and unemployed youth who were struggling for seeking means of livelihood, particularly in the underdeveloped rural areas saw a ray of hope in the appeal of the Maoists. This group of young people became committed to the objectives and programme of the Maoists. The Maoists by talking of gender and class equity attracted large number of women towards their movement. Maoists could build strong women cadres and each village in the Maoist affected area had a revolutionary women's organization. The Maoist slogans of dehinduaisation, anti-Brahminism, secular politics, abolition of caste and class hierarchies have been quite appealing to the ethnic communities particularly the Mongoloid communities. Therefore, a large number of ethnic Mongoloid youth joined the Maoist movement. Thus, the Maoists mobilized those sections of the Nepali society that were deprived, discriminated and depressed and were dissatisfied with the existing state of affairs.

Maoists had gained lot of sympathy among rural women because of their anti-liquor drives. They also raised voice against social abuses and many ill social practices in rural areas. Due to these reasons also, they earned sympathy from the rural people. Those who had faced hardships from the government, those who had been persecuted by the village officials, police authorities and banks also became sympathizers of the Maoist insurgents. They also gained sympathy from those people in the rural areas who were emancipated from the feudal bondage by them. Maoists took action in villages against local exploiters like village shop keepers, money lenders, suspected people, anti-social elements etc. In this way they tried to build confidence among the local people. It is, however, a different issue that later on Maoists themselves could not contain entry of anti-social elements within their cadres. As the Maoist movement became more violent this initial sympathy was lost due to the fear of Maoists.

It seems that the Maoists pretended to be a social movement aimed at bringing social transformation in the country. They looked of feudal nature of the Nepali society and said that there was a need to freed Nepalese people from feudal bondage. In fact, a social agenda was essential in order to strengthen their social bases and seek strength from the masses. They supported demands of ethnic groups because they knew that the ethnic groups were highly critical of the existing socio-political order in Nepal. They tried to gain support of ethnic Mongoloid by raising the issue of Hindu domination. This resulted in the convergence of the interest of Maoists and ethnic groups. Maoists thought that the monarchy was at the top of the feudal hierarchy and its protector. So unless the monarchy was not dispowered the feudal order will not be diminished. Hence, they relied on a political agenda to dislodge monarchy and declare Nepal a secular and Republican state. That way the ultimate aim of Maoists became to get hold of political power. This has confused many whether it was a social movement or a political one.

Post-1990 Political Conditions and the Maoist Movement

The post-1990 political processes and the prevailing socio–economic conditions in Nepal were important in the rise of Maoist movement. Maoists as a political strategist tried to incash the conditions in order to move further for the attainment of their political objectives.

It can be said that the political chaos that prevailed in the country in the years immediately following the establishment of democracy, created conditions for the rise of the Maoist movement. The outcome of the first general elections (May, 1991) was rather disappointing as Nepali Congress the largest party, recorded only a razor thin majority and formed a weak government. It was not very late that the conflict of leadership and contest for power began to take place within Nepali Congress and between different political parties. The intra-party conflicts became so prominent that Prime Minister G.P. Koirala had to resign and declare a mid-term poll in 1994.

Again, the performance of the political parties was more disappointing in the mid-term polls as none could secure the majority. The UML formed a minority government. The first communist government also failed due to inter-and intra-party cleavages and survived till mind 1995 only. The Nepali Congress again came to power in September 1995, with its second rank leadership Sher Bahadur Deuba at the helm of affairs but the party fluids continued. It was indeed the beginning of weak coalition and instable governments in Nepal. None of the incumbent governments could retain power even for a year.

Negligence on the part of the subsequent governments and the political parties on many counts generated widespread dissatisfaction.[33] The formation and reformation of governments proved to be a drama of power sharing and power grabbing. The functioning of the governments was marked by widespread corruption, favoritism and nepotism. On the other hand, government took strong actions against hardcore communists in many areas of western region, where they were active and had strong hold in the rural areas. In Rukum and Rolpa government launched Operation Romeo against the Maoists. Such types of actions by the Government indicated that it wanted to suppress the communist activists. It indeed gave an adverse message and the Maoists lost their faith on the government.

It was obvious that the government failed in addressing itself to the developmental issues. Nepal was characterized as one of the poorest country in the 1989 World Bank Report. Out of 120 countries it ranked 115. Nepal's per capita income was US $ 220. The UNDP Human Development Report 2001 stated that 38 per cent of Nepal's population was extremely poor and was not in a position to meet its basic requirements. There were widespread uneven distributions of income and wealth.[34] The democratic government instead of going for distributive justice strengthened these trends. There were sharp hill vis-à-vis Terai, urban-rural and caste divides in the distribution of land and economic benefits. There was over concentration of resources and wealth. Many regions were neglected in the distribution of resources and developmental programmes. This was the reason why Maoists concentrated in these regions to cultivate them for a movement.[35] It can be said that there were sufficient socio-economic and political reasons for giving way to an insurgency in Nepal.

The Maoist movement began in February 1996 in 6 districts of the Western development region. They soon entered into guerilla warfare against the government establishments. They raised their resources through different tactics and expanded the area of influence in the rural areas, where they ultimately installed their own parallel administration. The Maoists were declared terrorists and royal army was deployed to contain them in November 2001. Thus a war like situation began to take place in Nepal. It cost more than 13000 lives, huge economic losses and displacement of large number of people from the rural areas due to the fear of Maoists in the later half phase of the movement.

The Maoists followed a dynamic approach and adopted flexibility in their strategies. They agreed for a dialogue with the government (2001 & 2003) but did not compromise with their demands of a republican state and constituent assembly. The Maoists showed determination as far as their political objectives were concerned. Initially, Maoists gave enough consideration to fight against social rigidities, abuses, ill traditions problem of alcoholism and other such practices in rural areas. When the Maoists destroyed liquor shops and threw out all kinds of liquor from shops in the far–western Nepal it attracted the people a lot, particularly the women who had been a victim of alcoholism and ill social traditions. But after the royal army was deployed against the Maoists, the later had to concentrate more on the strategies to combat the royal army. They needed more resources and more support. There were lot of killings and arrests. The people, specially the younger generation who initially looked at Maoists as an alternative to their problems now started doubting over the ability of the Maoists to give a defeat to the royal army. The prolonged insurgency also added to the economic hardships of the people in many ways. The government of Nepal sought international arms assistance to flight against the Maoists. Thus the strength and capabilities of the royal army was on the increase.

All these factors made Maoists reactionary and violent. This added to the problems of the rural people. As a result Maoists started loosing their popularity in the rural areas. A large number of innocent people in the rural areas were also becoming a victim of the governmental administrations, because of arrests, intrigues, etc.

The Maoists though gave the impression that the socio-economic transformation is not possible in Nepal without a shift in the power structure of the country they failed in envisaging an alternative strategy to get hold of political power. It is true that they had a hold in the countryside in many areas but they hardly had any command of the urban areas. They also lacked any strategy to enter to the urban areas.

It seems that it is in view of these limitations that Maoists have agreed for an understanding with the seven party alliances to bring up a political transformation through constitutional means. The political transformation is still in its way and the social and economic transformation may only follow that.

Concluding Observations

On the whole one can observe a multi-dimensional discontent brewing up in the Nepalese society. The dalits and the ethnic groups have challenged the existing contours of Nepali state and society. They are looking for a space. The issues raised by dalits and ethnic groups are significant and a plural society like Nepal is bound to face these problems later or sooner. It is true that the dalit or the ethnic movements are still in a formative stage but the Nepali society can feel the smoke coming up. It is not possible to attain the goals of social cohesion unless these issues are properly addressed.

The Maoists movement should be viewed in a broader perspective here. Apart from its political overtones, the Maoist movement is a strong and violent reaction against the feudalistic and authoritarian approach of the Nepali society and polity. Whether or not the Maoist movement has come to an end whether or not the Maoists join the mainstream politics of Nepal they have left a lesson for the country that it will have to come out of the feudalistic order of the society. There is a need to look into the issues being raised by dalits, ethnic groups and the Maoists. There is also a need to take measures to resolve these issues with a long-term perspective of social equality, freedom and fraternity. One has to be cautious about politicization of dalits and ethnic groups. The regional issues are equally important in the context of nation-building.

A democratic system alone can address to the problems of depressed sections of the society. Thus the political democracy and the social democracy have to go hand in hand.

The social issues coming up in Nepal are, by and large, addressed to the state. So the major responsibility to resolve them lies with the state. However, in a democratic society it is not only the state that should take up the burden of social transformation. The civil society, political parties, groups, the intelligentsia, media all have a role to play in this regard.

Two more issues are important here: One is that the constitutional—legal measures alone are not sufficient to eradicate the traditional bonds of the society. A perceptional change is required at all levels in the society to realize goals of social parity. Secondly, no society can be transformed overnight. It has to be a gradual and continuous process. But there requires a clear perspective and a strong determination particularly on the part of the ruling elite of the country.

REFERENCES

1. Antony Arblaster, *Democracy,* World View Publications, Delhi, 1997: 8–9.
2. Jean Bachler, *Democracy, An Analytical Survey,* NBT, New Delhi, 1998: 74.

3. Jean Bachler, N. 2: 163.
4. For Instance see, J.S. Mill, *Representative Government*, J.M. Dent, London, 1976: 217.
5. Antony Arblaster, N. 1: 76.
6. Richard Burghart (ed.), *The Conditions of Listening, Essays on Religion, History and Politics in South Asia*, Oxford University Press, Delhi, 1996.
7. A. Hoffer, *The Caste Hierarchy and the State in Nepal. A Study of the Mulki Ani of 1854*, Innsbruk Unwersthitas–veriag, Wegner, 1979.
8. B.C. Upreti, "Monarchy and the Modernization in Nepal", in S.K. Chaube (ed.), *Modernization in the Himalayas*, Delhi, 1986.
9. Fredrick, H. Haige, *Regionalism and National Unity in Nepal*, California University Press, California, 1975.
10. Harka, B. Gurung, *Nepal, Social Demography and Expression*, New Era, Kathmandu, 1998: 88.
11. Harka, B. Gurung, "State and Society in Nepal", in David N. Gallner *et al.*, (eds.), *Nationalism and Ethnicity in a Hindu Kingdom: The Politics of Culture in Contemporary Nepal*, Harwood Academic Publications Amsterdam, 1997: 465-532.
12. See, Bhuwan Lal Joshi & Leo. E Rose, *Democratic Innovations in Nepal, A Case Study of Political Acculturation*, California University Press, California, 1965; Margaret W. Fisher and Leo E. Rose, *Politics of Nepal, Persistence and Change in Asian Monarchy*, Cornell, University Press, Ithaca, 1970.
13. For dalit movement and relate issue see, H. Kotari (ed.), Cate System untouchability and the Depressed, New Delhi, 1917.
14. See, Rishikeshav Raj Regmi, *Dimensions of Nepali Culture and Society*, SANN Research Institute, Kathmandu, 1990.
15. See, Hiralal Vishkarma, *A Strategy for the Upliftment and Empowerment of Dalits*, Action Aid Nepal, Kathmandu, 1996.
16. Dhrub K.C. *et al.*, "The problem of Disadvantaged people in caste society: An appraisal from Civil Society Perspective" in Khadga K.C. (ed.), The Institutionalisation of Democratic Polity in Nepal, FES, Kathmandu, 2000: 99–101.
17. N. 16: 103.
18. Yam Bahadur, *Nepal Ma Dalit Jatiya Mukti Andolan*, Kishan Jan Utthau Pratisthan, Kathmandu, 2002: 98–113.
19. Yam Bahadur, N. 18: 156–157.
20. See, Dor Bahadur Bisht, *People of Nepal*, Ratna Pushtak Bhandar, Kathmandu, 1970.

21. Urmila Phadnis, *Ethnicity and Nation–Building in South Asia*, Sage Publications, New Delhi, 1990: 123.
22. Dilli Ram Dahal, "Ethnic Calandron, Demography and Minority Politics: The Case of Nepal", in Dhrub Kumar (ed.), *State Leadership and Politics in Nepal*, CNAS, Kathmandu, 1995.
23. Krishna B. Bhattachan, "Ethno–Politics and Ethno-Development: An Emerging Paradigns in Nepal", in Dhrub Kumar (ed.), *State, Leadership and Politics in Nepal*, CNAS, Kathmandu, 1995: 123.
24. Praya Raj Sharma, *The State and Society in Nepal, Historical Foundations and Contemporary Trends*, Hindu Books, Kathmandu, 2004: 219.
25. *Nepali Patra* (Kathmandu), June 4, 1994.
26. N. 24: 222.
27. Ramakant and B.C. Upreti, "Regionalism in Nepal", Ramakant (ed.), *Regionalism in South Asia*, Aalekh Jaipur, 1984: 138–172.
28. *Saptahik Manch* (Kathmandu), June 28, 1990.
29. For reflections on Maoist movement see, Arjun Karki and David Seddon (eds.), *The People's War in Nepal*, Adroit Publishers, Delhi 2003, Deepak Thapa and Bandita Sijapati, *A Kingdom under Seige: Nepal's Maoist Insurgency*, The Printhouse, Kathmandu, 2003.
30. *Sapthaik Bimansha* (Kathmandu), March 22, 1996.
31. N. 30.
32. For the statement see, *Gorkhapatra* (Kathmandu), February 6, 1996.
33. Pancha N. Maharjan, "The Maoist Insurgency and Crisis of Governability in Nepal", in Dhrub Kumar (ed.), *Domestic Conflict and Crisis of Governability in Nepal*, CNAS, Kathmandu, 2000.
34. Deepak Thapa and Bandita Sijapati, N. 29: 59.
35. N. 29: 67.
36. Bhagirath Yogi, "The Cost of Insurgency, *New Business Age*, May, 2002.

6
Developmental Issues and Constraints

An inclusive democracy requires equitable development ensuring empowerment of weaker sections of the society, realization of popular needs and aspirations and providing basic needs to the people. It is possible when the economy of the country is developed to the extent that it satisfies the common man. A democratic system can be installed even in a backward and underdeveloped country. But democracy cannot be sustained there without a stable economy that is in a position to meet basic requirements of the people and provide sufficient opportunities to them on an equitable basis. It is in this context that the economic imperative of democracy becomes significant. Economic development is indeed essential for successful working of democracy. On the other hand, in a democracy it is essential that the basic needs of the people are met with. Thus the two are irreparable.

In this chapter our endeavour is to understand the nature and dynamics of the Nepali economy particularly in the last two decades. It is not possible here to make a comprehensive overview of Nepali economy. But the point that we would like to make here is that to what extent economy of Nepal has been supportive to the working of democracy.

The Inheritances

Nepal's economy was primarily static, backward and feudal to the core before 1950. The entire economy was controlled by a handful of persons belonging to the ruling class. No attempts were made by the Rana rulers to modernize the economy. In fact, it was in their interest to keep the country economically backward, so that they would not face any challenge.

The economy was predominantly agricultural. Approximately 94 per cent of the population was engaged in agriculture. Most of the land was owned by a handful of privileged class. It was also not well organized. The total area under cultivation was small. Only isolated and small pockets in the hills and Tarai were under cultivation through primitive methods of cultivation.

The cultivated land had been classified into five categories. Raikar (state ownership), Guthi (religious organization), Birta (individual ownership), Kipat (communal land ownership) and Jagir (assigned to individuals by the state).[1] The Birta and Jagir land systems were evolved by the Shah rulers in order to gain support from feudals for their authoritarian rule. Large chunks of agricultural land were given away as a reward to those who had rendered loyal service to the government. These land systems were retained during the Rana rule, but lands was confiscated from the possession of the old nobility and were reallotted to the members of the Rana families and its supporters.[2] It is estimated that during the Rana rule, nearly 95 per cent of the national wealth was possessed or controlled by the Ranas and the nobility.[3]

The size of land holding varied in different regions of the country. In the hills it was small and the productivity was very low because of harsh weather conditions and lack of modern agricultural technology.[4] In the Kathmandu valley the average land holding for a family varied from 2 to 1.5 acres. Land holding was comparatively larger in the Tarai region.[5] The landlords enjoyed absolute powers and farmers were dependent on them.

Nepal had a weak economic infrastructure before 1950. It had only 5 km of pitched road in all. Roads were mostly confined to the Kathmandu valley. A 84 km long narrow-gauge railway line was constructed from Raxaul to Amlekhganj in 1929.[6] It also had a 22 km ropeway from Dhading to Kathmandu. Because of lack of transport facilities people had to travel on foot in most parts of the country. At certain places it was more convenient to travel through the Indian Territory and then enter into Nepal at some other point. Goods were transported by animals or human beings. The postal and other communication services were inadequate and primitive.[7] In most parts of the country postal service were operated by foot carriers. The telephone system was introduced in 1916 but it was not available to the public till 1950. Electricity was unknown to the Nepalese before the twentieth century. In 1911, the first hydro-electric project of the country was installed at Sunderijal with a capacity of 900 KW electricity. Till 1956 Nepal's total hydro-electric output was 2150 KW.[8] The industrial development was almost non-existent. Some jute, cotton, match and cigarette factories were established in the Tarai region during the Second World War period but none functioned satisfactorily and had to be closed down. It is clear from this overview that Nepal had a very weak economic structure inherited from the Rana rulers in 1950. It was certainly not supportive the working of a democratic order.

Post-1950 Infrastructural Developments

Nepal moved on the path of modernization and development towards the middle of 1950's. Nepal's primary requirement was to build a viable economic infrastructure. Nepal's constraints were numerous such as, hilly topography by and large; no inheritance of economic infrastructure except an agriculture based rural economy, feudalistic order of socio-economy and the Asiatic mode of production; lack of capital, technological and human resources absence of market and landlocked nature of the country. It was clear that Nepal's aspirations of modernization and development could be met with by foreign aid alone. India and the United States had already started giving aid to Nepal and more and more countries opened their aid programmes in Nepal in the subsequent years. Nepal's heavy reliance on foreign aid still continues. Till mid-seventies Nepal gave more importance to infrastructure development. There is no doubt that Nepal has made a steady progress in many sectors. Some change is visible. However, it is difficult to state that Nepal has attained the goal of building a viable economic infrastructure. There are gaps, inadequacies and disparities in geographical terms. Nepal has spent 4 $ billion on infrastructural development works since 1956.[9] Till 2003, Nepal had a total road network of 15,905 km, while road transportation is the only viable means of travel in the country. There is a small railway network in Tarai. International and domestic air services are available in some parts. In some remote districts air strips are the only means of communication. However, their functionality depends on the weather conditions. Out of 75 districts 15 are yet not connected by roads. There are some districts particularly in western Nepal, where even the districts headquarter is not connected by a road to the rest of the country.[10]

Most of the areas of the country are now covered by telecommunication and postal services. However, these services are not adequate in some parts of the country. Moreover, in certain parts of the hill region people have to walk down a long way to avail of these facilities. Nepal has not been able to utilize its vast potential of river water resources for electricity generation and irrigation. Nepal is the second richest country of the world in river water resources with a capacity to generate 83,000 MW electricity. But the country is still short of electricity due to inadequate capital and technological resources.

Social Sector Development

Nepal has given much emphasis to the development of basic facilities for the people. In fact, for the broadening of the process of democracy it is necessary that more and more people are associated with the development process.

Nepal is struggling hard to provide educational facilities to all its people and regions of the country. The country is still lagging behind in this regard with 44 per cent adult literacy rate. The women literacy rate is yet below. The public sector expenditure on education has been between 3 to 3.5 per cent of GDP. Efforts have been made to establish a network of educational institutions at all levels in the whole country. It is not adequate and many remote hill areas are still left out. But one can state that a steady progress has been made. The Tenth Five-year Plan (2002–2007) has stipulated that it will be possible to provide education to all by the year 2015. With the present state of education in the country it appears to be a difficult target. However, one can state that Nepal is conscious of expanding the education system.

A number of international agencies such as DANIDA, World Bank, EU NORAD, UNICEF, etc., have been providing financial and other resources for educational expansion. A Basic Primary Education Programme was also launched with the assistance of international agencies.

After 1990 privatization of education has taken place. As a result a large number of private and boarding schools have been opened. These schools emphasize upon English as the medium of education so they are becoming more popular. However, the Maoists were not happy with the private educational institutions, due to which a large number of private institutions had to be closed down. Nepal has still to go a long way in attaining the goals of educational development.

It is essential in a democratic society to provide at least minimum health facilities to its people. However, the situation of health has been worst than that of education. It can be understood on the basis of the fact that the public sector expenditure on health has been one of the lowest in Nepal all over the world with only 1 to 1.5 per cent of GDP. There has been shortage of doctors and other medical staff. A large number of health centers and even hospitals are without doctors, particularly in the far western region of Nepal.[11] There is one doctor to every 15000 persons. This alone would speak of miserable situation of health facilities in the country. It has been estimated that Nepal needs to spent US $ 36 per capita to provide health facilities to its people, while the present per capita expenditure is somewhere near to 4 US $.[12] It shows that the health facilities are far behind the requirement of the country. A large number of Non-Governmental Organizations (NGO) are helping the people in cases related to health, health awareness programmes, vaccination and general medication. Nearly 234 NGO's were working in this field till 2002.

Development in the field of sanitation facilities and safe drinking water has also not been encouraging. 81 per cent of the population has access to drinking water facilities. But safe drinking water has been a serious problem even in Kathmandu. Only 27 per cent of the population has been using adequate sanitation facilities.

It can be said here that despite some headway, the social sector development is still at a primary stage.

Agriculture and Food Security

Nepal has a predominantly agriculture economy. It will be clear by the fact that 92 per cent population of the mountains, 84 per cent in the hills and 74 per cent in the Tarai is involved in agriculture. Nepal has a rural economy and nearly 88 per cent of the economy is agriculture based.[13]

Nepal has given top priority to the development of agriculture sector in its various development plans. However, the agriculture sector is still dependent on traditional means of cultivation and weather conditions. Only a small part of the land is under cultivation.[14] Only 0.5 per cent of the total land is under permanent crops and 38 per cent of the cropland is irrigated. The agriculture sector contributes to 40.6 per cent of GDP. The growth of agriculture production was 1.5 per annum between 1970–1985 which was lower than the rate of population growth.[15]

The food deficiency has been a serious problem in Nepal. It is in existence in a way, because of nominal growth in agriculture sector and high population growth rate. In 1995, 50 out of 75 districts were food deficit. During 1997–98, there was a food deficit of 150729 MT and it was 60,385 MT during 1999–2000. In the remote mountainous regions there is not only the problem of food deficiency but the supply of food to these regions is a big problem. There are no means of transportation and the only way to supply food grains is hill animals or porters. Certain modest attempts were made for the development of the economy. In this regard Nepal's main challenges were non-availability of capital and technological knowhow for building an economic infrastructure. As a result it had to depend on foreign aid from various sources. It was expected that with the help of foreign aid the country would be able to mobilize its own resources and thus attain a certain level of economic growth.

Planned Development

Nepal's quest for modernization and development received a concrete shape and direction with the launching of the First Five-Year Plan in 1956. Although the Plan was totally dependent on foreign assistance, it aimed at laying a sound foundation of infrastructural development in the country. Since Nepal lacked basic facilities, it obviously stressed upon infrastructural development. As such most of the plan investments were made in non-productive areas. The development of transport and communication acquired prominence. This trend continued till 1975.

After 1975 (Fifth Plan) Nepal changed its strategy and began to lay emphasis on the development of productive areas. There were two reasons behind it. Firstly, there had been over-concentration on infrastructural development so far and it had become an issue of criticism. Actually it had failed in providing immediate relief to the people. Secondly, after 1975 the foreign aid structure also underwent a change. The donor agencies were also emphasizing on the development of productive sectors, so Nepal had to follow this trend.

Nepal also followed a social mobilization approach in order to achieve targets of the various five year plans, as well as, to encourage process of modernization and development in the social sector. In 1975, Small Farmers Development Programme was launched with a view to help small farmers. In 1991, a fifth development region was constituted named as mid-western region. The basic idea behind re-division the country on the basis of development regions had been to shift the focus from geographic regions to development regions. It also aimed at reducing regional disparities. Actually the western region has been the most backward part of the country. So a new development region was created in order to focus on the problems of that area more intensively.

In the Seventh Plan it was estimated to increase GDP by 4.5 per cent per annum. The agriculture sector was projected to grow at an annual rate of 3.5 per cent and non-agriculture sector at 5.7 per cent.[16] However, Nepal has not been able to mobilize its own capital resources for its development plans.[17] As a result, its dependence on foreign aid has continued. It has not succeeded so far in fully achieving the directives of various plans. In the 9th Plan (1998–2002) it was proposed to reduce poverty. The total plan outlay amounted to Rs. 66 billion.

In the Tenth Five-Year Plan (2002–2007) as well poverty reduction programme has been emphasized. It is proposed to bring down the level of poverty to 30 per cent. There is also emphasis on setting a reform and investment programme in order to achieve higher economic growth rate and promote basic needs. It is difficult to state how near Nepal is this target in the prevailing conditions within the country.

Regional Disparities

Nepal's three geographic regions, which exhibit strong ecological variations also, have different levels of development. The Tarai people have been subject to discrimination in comparison to people of the hills. The mountains are resource-scarce regions. Similarly hills are poorly developed in comparison to Tarai and mountains are much less developed in comparison to the hills. Thus, there have been strong regional disparities in terms of resource, sand development potential, etc.

In order to avoid the hills vis-a-vis Tarai controversy and also in order to overcome regional disparities, a Regional Development Strategy was evolved in 1971. The new regional development plan was designed in such a manner that the identity of mountains, hills and Tarai could be dissolved. The country was divided into four development regions vertically. Each region constituted parts of hills, mountains and Tarai. These four regions were eastern development region, central development region, western development region and far-western development region. Later on, another region, the mid-western development region was also constituted. However, these approaches to development focused regions in place of geographic regions have not been able to eliminate regional disparities. In fact, the divisions between hills vis-a-vis Tarai are deep rooted. There have been regional imbalances in development programme and due to the hill domination the people of Tarai have suffered a lot. It can be said that the regional development approach failed in reducing regional disparities. Apart from the developmental constraints there are social and political regions behind regional disparities.

A Grameen Bank approach was followed. In 1994, Village Development Bank programme was launched. It was aimed at holistic development of the rural areas. Similarly, Sustainable Community Development Programme was also launched. In 1999 Women Empowerment and Income Generating Programme was also launched. It is clear that Nepal has launched a number of programmes along with the five-year plans so as to uplift the backward sections of the society such as women, people below poverty line, etc. It is a different question as to what extent social mobilization has taken place with the help of these programmes. But it shows an increased awareness and the efforts made by the democratic government. It may also be pointed out here that after the 1990 political change in Nepal, a large number of national and international Non-Governmental Organizations are active in the country and they have been working for the social and economic upliftment of the under-privileged sections of the society. This indicates that there is some sort of mobilization towards activating development in various ways. There are problems as well. Resources are not adequately available. There is widespread corruption and bureaucratic delays and so on. Yet it can be said that there is an increased awareness in terms of developmental issues.

Industrial Development

The country is still very poor in the field of industrial development. It was only during the mid-sixties that some steps were taken towards industrial development. The lack of infrastructural facilities, capital, technology and poor accessibility to domestic and international markets low purchasing power of the people etc., have been the root cause of slow place of industrial development. It may also be pointed out here that the whole landscape of the country is not suitable to industrial development, particularly heavy industrialization is not possible in the hills and mountains due to harsh climatic conditions, lack of availability of resources and domestic market as well as shortage of skilled and unskilled labour. In the Himalayan region industrialization is not possible due to the above stated reasons. In the hill areas only big valleys such as the Kathmandu and Pokhara valley have the infrastructural facilities available for industrial development. The small stretch of Tarai towards south is suitable for the establishment of industries.

Another important aspect is that, by and large, medium and small-scale industrialization has come up in Nepal and heavy industrialization is still at an infant stage.[18] It has not been possible to provide large-scale employment in the industrial sector, due to the small size of industrial sector. Similarly the contribution of industrial sector to GDP has also been poor. Till 1994-95 there were altogether 4487 industrial establishments in the country, which provided employment to 243,922 persons.

Gender Development

The gender equality is an essential component of a democratic order. In fact, in modern times the project of democracy cannot be completed unless the objective of gender equity is not attained. It is now realized that the level of civilization of a country is best judged by the status that women are accorded in the society. It is generally assumed that most of the countries of the third world are in a transitional phase as far as the question of status of women is concerned. The women have been subject to discriminations, ill-treatment and underdevelopment owing to social and religio-cultural traditions, attitudes and perception, male chauvinisms, discriminatory developmental policies, etc. The issues involved in the empowerment of women are social status and recognition, literacy, rights, health, adequate representation to women in services, politics and other walks of life and denouncing the social and religion based discriminations against women. The empowerment of women is thus equitable distribution of resources, power and status in political, social and economic realm.[19]

In Nepal the issue of empowerment of women is being addressed properly only in the last few decades. The condition of women particularly in the rural hills is quite miserable. Nepal ranks 116 among the countries of the world in terms of the gender related index. Women constitute slightly more than half (50.05%) of the total population of the country. The female adult literacy rate is 26.4 per cent, which is quite low. In fact, Nepal has a lower status in terms of female literacy.[20] Women are largely engaged in agriculture. The women employment is largely characterized by low skilled sectors, subsistence work orientation and low paid jobs.

The Nepali women are most disadvantaged. In the social hierarchy the status of women is generally much lower. However, it has to be understood that there are sharp variations as well, in this regard among the Mongoloid Communities and the other tribal people. In some communities women have an equitable or higher status as well. However, in general women lag far behind men in access to education, resources and ownership rights. In nutshell it can be said that:

1. It is difficult for women to move to other sectors of employment than agriculture work due to low literacy, training and skills.
2. It is difficult for women to raise their own capital because they cannot own land and also due to unfavourable property rights and inheritance laws.
3. Social customs, traditions, religious norms are still a binding force for women.
4. As the women are left to own all kinds of household responsibilities due to large scale out migration of men folks, their problems are multiplied.
5. There are serious problems of violence against women and trafficking in children.

6. The legislative measures though not so adequate in Nepal are not sufficient; there is a need for perceptional and attitudinal change in the Nepalese society in favour of women.

Poverty and Unemployment

Poverty is a major challenge to the Nepalese economy. Nearly 42 per cent of the total population lives below poverty line. Poverty is more in the rural areas in comparison to the population. In geographical terms the mid-western and far-western regions are poorer compared to the national average. What is striking about Nepal is that its percentage of people below poverty line has not changed over the last 3 decades.[21] One reason behind this consistency could be Nepal's population growth rate that has been higher to the annual growth in economy.

There are vast inequalities existing in the Nepalese society. These inequalities can be observed in terms of income, standard of life and consumption patterns. Nearly 37.7 per cent of the population has an income less than one dollar a day. The poorest 10 per cent of the population consumes 3.2 per cent resources. The poorest 20 per cent consume 44.8 per cent and the richest 10 per cent consume 29.8 per cent resources. Thus 30 per cent population consumes 75 per cent of the resources. The Ninth Five-Year Plan (1998–2002) of the country emphasized poverty reduction by 10 per cent by the end of the plan. But this target was hardly visible anywhere because of faculty implementation of various programmes, absence of a comprehensive framework and poor governance. The Tenth Five-Year Plan (2002-2007) also accorded top priority to poverty reduction from 40 to 30 per cent by the financial year 2007. Based on the 10th Plan priority government announced its poverty reduction strategy in 2003. Some of the policy measures that were emphasized included improved delivery of basic services, promotions to social inclusion, implementation of targeted programmes for poor and disadvantaged groups etc.

The problem of unemployment and under employment is acute in Nepal. Agriculture is the only sector that has capacity to provide large scale employment. But in the hills and mountains agriculture does not provide employment to all and for the whole year. The service and industries sectors do not provide enough employment opportunities. In tourism and trade and commerce sectors situation has remained fluctuating over the years due to the insurgency. Therefore, the problem of unemployment has increased further. In 2000 the rate of unemployment was less than 2 per cent but more than 7 per cent in the urban areas.

Nepal continues to depend on foreign aid and foreign loans for its development projects. Nearly 65 per cent of the development projects were financed by foreign grants or loans in the 1990's, while it was 50 per cent in the previous years. Yet another problem has been its increasing trade deficit. In 2000 Nepal's trade deficit was US $ 766 million, which increased to 1141 million US $ in 2005. The increased defence expenditure is also a matter of concern for Nepal. It has proved to be a major stumbling block to the growth of Nepali economy. In 1985 Nepal's defence expenditure was 22 million US $ in 2002. The defence expenditure constituted 8.6 per cent of Nepal's total government expenditure in 2002.

GDP Position

Nepal's gross domestic production has not gone above 6.0 per cent for last one decade between 1997-06. Only in 2000 GDP rose to 6.00 per cent. This could be due to favourable climatic conditions that gave boost to agriculture production. Otherwise the political climate was not suitable for any upward swing of the economy. Tear 2002 was worst in terms of GDP growth rate as it showed a negative trend with –0.4 per cent GDP. The next year too was not encouraging as the GDP remained at 2.6 per cent. These were indeed troubled years for Nepal due to political stability, rise of authoritarian trends and the Maoist insurgency. After 2003 there have been some signs of improvement with 4.0 per cent in 2004 and 5.0 per cent in 2005. It can be said here that with this GDP rate Nepali economy cannot meet its goals and requirements. It can also be said that the political environment plays an important role in the upward mobility of the economy. It may also be noted here that Nepal's per capita GNP has been between US $ 230 - 250 over the years, which is also very low.

Concluding Observations

Nepal's economy is till largely traditional with heavy dependence on pastoral agriculture. Efforts towards development have been rather ad hoc instead of being planned and based on objective conditions. The transformation of the economy is slow and inadequate. The main problems of Nepali economy are:

High population growth rate

Low economic growth rate

Inadequate infrastructural developments

Resource gap

Unemployment

Poverty

Regional disparities

Income inequalities

Aid dependence

Foreign debt burden

Trade imbalance and trade deficit

Rising living cost

Nepal needs to recast its priorities and lay thrust on the development of core areas of economy in a long-term perspective. Nepal's primary concern has to be on reduction in population growth rate. Unless it is done no substantial growth in economy is possible. In the present circumstances Nepal's sustained growth would require revitalization of agriculture sector. It needs modern inputs to agriculture sector so that its dependence on weather conditions is required. Along with intensive modernization of agriculture there is a need for a reform agenda. Nepal also needs effective domestic revenue collection, improved economic supervision capabilities and financial management. This needs reforms in administrative structure. There is also need for mobilization of domestic resources so that external dependence could be minimized. Political stability and democratic governance is of course, a must for the sustainable economic growth.

REFERENCES

1. For a detailed discussion see, Mahesh C. Regami, *Land Ownership in Nepal,* California University Press, Berkeley, 1975.
2. Mahesh C. Regani, *Thatched Hutts and Stuckoo Palaces: Peasants and Landlords in 19th Century Nepal,* New Delhi, 1978.
3. D.R. Regami, *Whither Nepal,* Lucknow, 1957.
4. M.C. Regami, *A Study in Nepali Economic History,* New Delhi, 1971: 198.

5. E. Rauch, *Report to the Government of Nepal on Farm Enterprises*, Food and Agriculture Organisation, UNO, 1954; 6.
6. For details see, Shrestha, *An Introduction to Nepalese Economy*, Ratna Pustak Bhandar, Kathmandu, 1981; Navin C. Joshi, *Readings in Nepalese Economy*, Chugh Publications, Allahabad; 1978.
7. *First Five-Year Plan* (1950-61) HMG, Kathmandu, 1956: 49- 50.
8. Progress Report, First Five-Year Plan, *National Planning Commission*, HMG, Kathmandu, 1961: 74.
9. Diwakar Chand, *Essays on Development of Nepal*, Chandni Publications, Kathmandu, 2003: 132.
10. See for a comprehensive study, B.C. Upreti, *Nepal, Dilemmas of Development and Change in Far-Western Hills*, India, New Delhi, 2006.
11. B.C. Upreti, N. 10.
12. Diwakar Chand, N. 9: 160.
13. See, Y.P. Pant and S.C. Jain, *Long-term Planning for Agriculture in Nepal*, Vikas, Delhi, 1972.
14. "A Review of Nepal's efforts in Poverty Alleviation", *Food and Agriculture Organisation*, Indepth Studies Series, No. 13, 1983.
15. *Population Monograph of Nepal*, Central Bureau of Statistics, HMG, Kathmandu, 1987.
16. *Seventh Five-Year Plan, National Planning Commission*, HMG, Kathmandu.
17. See, Hari Bans Jha, *Resource Mobilisation and Economic Development in Nepal During the Plan Period*, Allahabad, 1984.
18. See, Laurie Zivetz, *Private Enterprise and the State in Modern Nepal*, Oxford University Press, New Delhi, 1991.
19. J. Rowlands, *Questioning Empowerment*, Oxford, 1897.
20. *Asian Development Outlook*, ADB, New York, 2001: 121.
21. Divakar Chand, N. 9: 136.

Table–I
Main Economic Indicators

1.	GDP (US $ billion 2002	5.5
2.	GDP Per capita (PPP US $) 2002	1370
3.	GNP Per capita US $ 2002	230
4.	Income share ratio of highest 20% to lowest 20% 1995–2000.	5.9
5.	Population below income poverty line (%) ($ 1 a day (1993 ppp US $) 1990-02)	37.7
6.	National Poverty like 1990–01	42.0
7.	Population below income poverty line % 1995–2000 Urban	23.0
	Rural	44.0
8.	Public expenditure on education (as % of GDP 1999–01)	3.4
9.	Public expenditure on health (as % of GDP 200)	1.5
10.	Gross capital formation (as % of GDP 2002)	25
11.	Gross domestic savings (as % of GDP 2002)	12
12.	Industry value added (as % of GDP 2002)	22
13.	Exports (as % of GDP 2002)	16
	Total debt secure (as % of exports of goods and Services 2002)	8.8
	Total ODI 2002	
	US $ mn.	366
	As % of GDP	6.7
	Total external debt—US $ billion 2002	2953

Source: Various Reports of *Human Development Report, South Asia*, Oxford University Press, Karachi, Pakistan.

Table–II
Human Development Indicators: Population and Education

1.	Total population 2002	25 mn.
2.	Annual Population growth 1997–02 (%)	2.3
3.	Life Expectancy at birth (2002)	60 years
4.	Adult literacy rate 15 years above 2002 (%)	44

(Contd.)

5.	Female literacy rate (15 years and above 2002 (%)	26
6.	Infant Mortality rate 2002 (per 1000 live birth)	66
7.	Public expenditure on education (as percentage of GDP) 1 960	0.4
	1999–2001	3.4

Source: *Human Development in South Asia* 2004, Oxford University Press, Karachi, 2005.

Table–III
Trends in Defence Expenditure

1.	Defence Expenditure (US $ mn. 1999 prices	1985	22.0
		2002	90.0
2.	Defence Expenditure annual increase between 1985–2002 (percentage)		8.6
3.	Defence Expenditure (as percentage of GDP)	1985	0.7
		2002	1.4
4.	Defence expenditure as percentage of government expenditure	1985	6.7
		2002	8.6
5.	Defence expenditure per capita (US $ 1999 prices)	1985	1.3
		2002	3.7
6.	Armed forces in thousands	1985	25
		2002	51

Source: *Human Development in South Asia* 2004, 2005: 257.

Table–IV
Expenditure on Development and Security

S.No.	*Year*	*Development*	*Security*
1.	1997	9.8	1.9
2.	1998	9.9	1.9
3.	1999	8.1	1.9
4.	2000	8.1	1.9
5.	2001	8.5	2.0
6.	2002	7.8	2.4
7	2003	6.0	2.5

Source: *Asian Outlook*, Oxford University Press, New York, 2004: 129.

Table–V
Major Economic Indicators 1997–05 (per cent)

S. No.	*Indication*	*1997*	*1998*	*1999*	*2000*	*2001*	*2002*	*2003*	*2004*	*2005*
1	GDP Growth	5.0	2.3	3.3	6.0	4.6	-0.4	2.6	4.0	5.0
2	Gross domestic Investment/GDP	25.3	20.7	17.3	24.2	23.8	25.6	26.9	25.5	25.0
3.	Gross domestic savings/GDP	12.1	9.5	10.6	18.8	19.0	-	-	-	-
4.	Inflation rate (Consumer price index)	7.8	4.0	12.7	3.5	2.4	2.9	4.8	4.5	5.0
5.	Money supply (MZ) growth	11.9	21.9	20.9	21.8	15.2	-4.4	8.1	9.3	11.0
6.	Fiscal balance/ GDP	-5.1	-6.0	-6.1	-3.3	-4.5	-3.9	-1.8	-2.7	-4.5
7.	Merchandise export growth	10.2	11.9	20.3	37.5	4.6	-20.3	-14.9	10.0	12.0
8.	Merchandise import growth	21.7	-12.4	-10.5	22.0	-0.2	-15.3	8.1	10.0	12.0
9.	Current account balance/GDP	-06.7	-5.5	-3.5	-5.3	-5.4	4.2	1.8	1.0	0.5
10.	Debt service exports	4.5	6.1	6.5	6.0	6.8	9.3	11.4	9.0	9.0

Source: Asian Development Outlook 2000-2004.

7

Political Issues and the Challenges of Democratic Stability

We have already made this point clear that the structural foundations constitute one vital aspect of the working of democracy in a country. It is equally important how the democratic system operates. In the operationalisation of democracy the issues that become important are the stability of government and its working, the role of political parties, the political perception, role and behaviour of individuals, groups and institutions, etc. This chapter intends to focus upon some of these issues. Our endeavour here will be to understand to what extent the political structures, groups and institutions working within the framework of a democratic political order proved to be supportive to democracy in Nepal.

Problems of Governmental Stability and Continuity

The stability of the government is a primary factor in building strong structural foundations of democracy in a country. The frequent changes in the governments results in the instability of the government, thereby posing challenges to democracy. The instability of government may result in the strengthening of bureaucracy there by giving rise to the dominating attitude of bureaucracy, government's inability in delivering goods to the people, frequent changes and alterations in the policies and programmes of the government lack of vision etc., weak leadership, increase in corruption and decreased popular faith and support to the government. It is thus clear that the governmental instability is a curse upon democracy. In fact, one has to be reminded here that the installation of democracy itself is no guarantee of its sustenance. Yet, another important aspect is that a democratic system is not a static system it needs to change itself and adjust accordingly with the changes in the circumstances. The sustenance of democracy in a long-term requires realization of popular needs and aspirations, long-term developmental policies and programmes and strong foundations of participatory democracy. It is possible only when there is governmental stability and continuity. The instability of government also reflects on the instability of governance. This has only resulted in the transitional nature of democracy.

Nepal's major problem in the last one and half decades has been governmental instability. An overview of the major shifts of government would clearly reflect that it has not been possible in Nepal to lay a strong foundation of democracy due to the frequent changes and instability of governments.

First Nepali Congress Government

The Nepali Congress constituted the first elected government after the 1990 election. The new government had the task to realize the aspirations of the people and the objectives of the 1990 democratic movement. Not only that the Nepali Congress Government had the responsibility to lay down a strong foundation of democracy, but it was also that there was an imperative need to activate the developmental process in the kingdom in order to realize popular needs and aspirations and also the successful working of democracy. The Koirala government decided to concentrate upon the following as thrust areas of its activities:

1. Free education for all up to secondary level.
2. Abolition of dual ownership of land.
3. Welfare of squatters and landless people.
4. Establishment of health centers in the rural areas.
5. Linking each district headquarters by road transportation.
6. Providing communication facilities in the rural areas.
7. Initiating the process of privatization and liberalization.

The Nepali Congress party was quite excited with its coming to power after a long gap. Hence, it wanted to adopt popular measures in order to strengthen its base. However, it was not an easy task for the party. There were serious problems within the party itself. The Bhattarai faction was not happy with the leadership of Koirala.[1] The organizational and the governmental wings of the party were opposed to each other. The Koirala faction on the one and the

Bhattarai–Ganesh Man Singh faction on the other hand were engaged in a serious leadership clash. Bhattarai lost the prestigious 1994 Kathmandu by-election, and it was blamed that he lost the by-election because of the non-cooperation of some of the party leaders. This widened the gap between the two factions of the party. Koirala was accused of ignoring the party organization in taking important policy decisions. He was also criticized by its own party men for being ineffective in the disposition of governmental functions.

The opposition political parties took advantage of the internal differences of the Nepali Congress party. The UML and the Unity Centre opposed the government on the issues of civil servants strike, Tanakpur barrage agreement with India, price rise of essential commodities, etc. The interest of the UML and the Bhattarai group within the Nepali Congress coincided and they began to pressurize the Koirala government to step down. There were indications that the UML and the anti-Koirala group within the Nepali Congress could unite together to pressurize the government in the house of re-presentatives. Towards the middle of 1994, there were also rumours that the non-confidence motion would be tabled against the government. Taking these developments into consideration, Koirala resigned in August 1994, before the motion could have been registered. The parliament was dissolved on his recommendation and fresh elections were declared. Thus, came an end to the first elected government. It was indeed not an encouraging development. The period of the first elected government was marked by party vis-a-vis government tussles, leadership clashes, oppositional politics and non-performance by the Government. While sincere efforts should have been made towards the strengthening of democracy, the functioning of the elected government resulted in political instability and disorder. In fact, the problems had started soon after the formation of the government. Koirala failed in taking the organization wing into confidence. Actually the organizational set up was with Bhattarai who was the president of the party.

The Communists in Power

In the mid-term elections of 1994, none of the contesting political parties could secure a majority. The UML emerge as the largest party with 88 seats and the Nepali Congress remained number two with 83 seats. The NDP secured 20 seats and the NSP 3. The UML formed a minority government under the leadership of Man Mohan

Adhikari with the support of NDP and other smaller political parties from outside. The Nepali Congress remained in the opposition.

It was for the first time in the history of Nepal that the Communists had got an opportunity to form the government. Although it was a minority government, there were speculations regarding the possible course of politics in the country. Lot of policy changes and new directions were being expected due to the position taken by the communists earlier, when they were not in power.[2] However, once the UML government started functioning these speculations proved to be false, as there was not much difference in the orientation of the communist government. However, the UML government formulated some popular programmes such as "Build Our Village Ourselves" (BOVO) programme, allowance (Rs.100) to old people, welfare programme for the landless and depressed communities, development of health facilities and irrigation facilities. The UML tried to strengthen its position in the rural areas. It also wanted party's domination in various government bodies. Hence, it made a large number of appointments from the party cadres in the government bodies, commissions, embassies, etc. Despite being a minority government it also took steps towards politicization of media, educational institutions and higher positions in the administration. As a result, the UML government invited opposition from the Nepali Congress, NDP and NSP. Nevertheless, the UML government could not initiate any fundamental change in the spheres of domestic and foreign policies of Nepal. The working of the government was also not much changed from the previous regime. Neither the government could impress any kind of social transformation in Nepal which was much required.

Nepali Congress Again in Power

In May 1995 the opposition political parties decided to move a non-confidence motion against the UML government. Prime Minister Man Mohan Adhikari resigned and recommended dissolution of the Parliament in the same way as G.P. Koirala had done earlier in 1994. The Parliament was dissolved and the King declared fresh elections. However, his decision was challenged in the Supreme Court and the Supreme Court ordered reinstallation of the Parliament. It was argued that before the Prime Minister had recommended dissolution of the parliament, the non-confidence motion had already been registered against the government. Hence, his request was not valid. The parliament was revived in September 1995. The Nepali Congress formed the government under the leadership of Sher Bahadur Deuba with the support of NDP and RPP. This time the Nepali Congress decided to handover Prime Ministership to the second rank leadership as there were strong differences among the top leadership of the party.

It was for the first time that the Nepali Congress agreed to form government with National Democratic Party (NDC), a party that had been labeled as the pro-panchayat party as its leaders belonged to the panchayat era leadership. But it seems that now NC was more interested in power than its ideological commitment. The NC, NDP, NSP coalition agreed upon a programme which included the following:

- To strengthen democratic norms and values based on constitutional monarchy and parliamentary system.
- Sustainable development.
- Adopting a balanced foreign policy.
- Encouragement to private sector in development.
- Utilisation of water resources through bilateral, multilateral and regional cooperation, keeping the national interest in top priority.
- Making villages as the focal point of developments of all kinds.
- Depoliticisation of educational institutions including universities.
- Respect to liberty, integrity and freedom of media.
- Arrangements to provide citizenship to all those born and were residing in Nepal.
- Launching a specific programme to uplift the living standard of the backward and deprived sections of the society, including Janajati and Madhesi community.

Era of Instable Coalition Governments

There is no doubt that the coalition government launched an impressive programme but there was hardly any time for the government to concentrate on these and other developmental and welfare issues. Sher Bahadur Deuba faced strong opposition from his own party as well as the UML. Actually though Deuba was a compromise candidate among the top leadership of the party, he was believed to be closer to K.P. Bhattarai. Hence, Koirala group was not happy with the government. Deuba government was charged with corruption and inefficiency. The Maoist insurgency had begun by this time and his government was also criticized for being unconcerned to the Maoist problem. The Deuba government survived a non-confidence motion in March 1996. But Deuba had to step down in March 1997.

In March 1997, the UML-NDP and NSP formed another coalition government under the leadership of Lokendra Bahadur Chand of NDP. This coalition could not survive for more than six months. This coalition government was replaced by another coalition of UML–NDP–NSP under the leadership of Surya Bahadur Thapa of NDP. Interestingly both Lokendra Bahadur Chand and Surya Bahadur Thapa of NDP enjoyed Prime Ministership with only 19 seats in the parliament. The Thapa government started facing strong opposition from the Nepali Congress and Thapa had to quit in April 1998. It was hardly possible for these coalition governments to concentrate on developmental programmes or build a consensus on National Issues.

The Nepali Congress again began to search possibilities for the formation of a new coalition government. Incidentally towards the end of 1997 after the local bodies elections, the UML had splitted with 40 MPs of UML under the leadership of Bam Deo Gautam and C.P. Mainali to form a new political party, called CPN-ML. The Nepali Congress and ML reached to an understanding to form a coalition government. While the NC was in search of a new partner the ML wanted to enhance its position against the UML. G.P. Koirala became the Prime Minister. The understanding was that the Prime Minister-ship would go to the other coalition partner after six months. In December 1998 Koirala refused to handover Prime Ministership to the ML. The two partners also developed differences over several other issues as well. The ML issued a 25 point programme which included increase in ML members in the cabinet, Kalapani issue, etc. Prime Minister Koirala did not accept these demands. 13 ML members of the cabinet resigned on 10th December 1998. The ML decided to table a motion of no confidence against the Koirala government. The UML came to the rescue of Nepali Congress not because it was willing to support the party but mainly because it wanted to let down the ML. Koirala resigned, the parliament was dissolved and fresh elections were declared for May 1999. The NC-ML-NSP formed a national government till the elections were held.

The coalition experiment was the bitterest experience in Nepalese politics. It was not only resulted in political instability but also reduced the prospects for the strengthening of democracy in the country. There were a large number of problems with the coalition government and their partners.

- The partner political parties in coalition governments lacked proper coordination and understanding.
- Almost in all the coalition governments each constituent political party acted individually.
- Each of the coalition partners tried to fit their own men in different organizations. They followed a kind of a spoil system.
- The political parties were confined to short-term personal gains. They were not concerned about long-term and national issues. None seemed concerned about the process of institutionalization of democracy.
- The coalition governments had hardly any time to address themselves to the socio-economic issues and popular needs and aspirations.
- The coalition partners lacked any ideological similarities. In fact most of the coalitions were misfit in ideological terms. Hence, it appeared that most of them were engaged in a power game. There only motive was to remain in power by whatever means it was possible. Each political party engaged in a coalition wanted to accumulate more powers. It however, resulted in the failure of coalition governments.

Second Phase of Governmental Instability

In the 1999 elections the Nepali Congress emerged as the wining party with 110 seats, UML as the main opposition party with 67 seats, NDP 11, NSP 5, Jana Morcha 5, United Jana Morcha 1 and NMKP 1 seats each. Interestingly, as discussed earlier, the ML could not register victory on a single seat. K.P. Bhattarai won the first election of his life and as per internal understanding of the party he became the leader of the parliamentary party. K.P. Bhattarai formed the government.

It was not very late that the Bhattarai government began to face criticism from its own party cadres. The Bhattarai government was charged for ineffectiveness, indifferent attitude towards the Maoist problem, etc. Since December 1999 the Koirala group began to oppose the Bhattarai government. They started pressurizing K.P. Bhattarai to resign from the government. The Koirala group ultimately threatened that if Bhattarai had not tendered his resignation a non-confidence motion was to be tabled against his government. Bhattarai resigned in February 2000. Thus, the pressure tactics of the Koirala group proved to be successful. But the things were not as smooth for Koirala as they used to be earlier. Sher Bahadur Deuba also claimed for the leadership of the parliamentary party. The tangle between Koirala and Deuba had to be resolved through voting in which Koirala won by 69 votes against 43 in favour of Deuba. G.P. Koirala became Prime Minister in March 2000. This phase of Koirala's Prime Ministership was marked by a number of developments. His government was charged for widespread corruption. The Maoist problem had been aggravated further by this time. Koirala government could not take up concrete steps towards the resolution of the problem. On June 1, 2001 King Birendra and his whole family was assassinated. The Koirala government was accused of being cool on this issue. The opposition political parties were also targeting Koirala.

Koirala had to resign in July 2001, and Sher Bahadur Deuba took over as the Prime Minister of the Nepali Congress government. Deuba was serious about the resolution of the Maoist problem. Earlier also he had headed a committee constituted during the tenure of Prime Minister Bhattarai for the resolution of the Maoist problem. Prime Minister Deuba persuaded the Maoist for a ceasefire and to bring them to the negotiation table between August–November 13, 2001.

The talks failed and on 26 November, 2001 a state of emergency were declared in Nepal. The army was called to bring the Maoists under control. The emergency was extended in February and May 2002. Deuba no doubt made sincere efforts towards the resolution of the Maoist problem. But there was no agreement on the basic issues. None of the parties were prepared to compromise. In May 2002 Deuba resigned and the parliament was dissolved. The fresh elections were to be held in November 2002 on a phased basis. Before the fresh elections could take place King Gyanendra dismissed Deuba in October 2002. Actually, in October Deuba had suggested that due to the Maoist insurgency it was not possible to hold general elections in time. In fact, it was being suggested that the elections could be postponed for sometime. But the King did not agree to the Prime Minister's suggestion and dismissed him.

After the dismissal of the elected government, King Gyanendra nominated Lokendra Bahadur Chand of NDP as Prime Minister with a small cabinet. The larger parties like Nepali Congress and UML did not join the government. King himself assumed the responsibility to revive the democratic process. He began to play an active role in politics. The failure of talks between the Maoists and the government in the middle of 2003 lead to the departure of Lokendra Bahadur Chand and Surya Bahadur Thapa was appointed as the new Prime Minister of Nepal. Despite their appearance and eclipse at many times King Gyanendra relied on the same set of political elite. It was obvious that the major political parties would not have lend their support to these governments. In the beginning of 2004 Thapa was being opposed by his own party members to the extent that it was being threatened to expel him from party. Thapa was also removed from the Prime Ministership after sometime and Sher Bahadur Dueba was appointed as the new Prime Minister. These changes further reduced the efficiency of the government. The parliament had already begun suspended, Maoists problem continued, the political parties were in a non-cooperative mood. King Gyanendra find these conditions appropriate to take powers in his hand. In February 2005 King Gyanendra terminated the Deuba government and took all powers in his hand. This time he brought in old timers like Tulsi Giri to help him in the administration. The King though succeeded in realizing his political ambitions for a while but it also lead to a process of polarization of democratic forces against him.

It is clear that for nearly one and half a decade Nepal has seen an era of unsuccessful governments, instability and ill governance. It was hardly possible and hardly expected from the short phased coalition governments that they would strengthen working of democratic institutions and stabilizes democracy in the country.

Political Parties and Democracy

Political parties are considered to be the backbone of a democratic system. The functioning of democratic institutions depends on the political parties. The structure of party system, their organizational and ideological base, leadership quality and commitment of democracy would determine the viability of a democratic system.

Thus, political parties provide dynamism to democracy. Democracy can survive in long-term only when there is a strong party system.[3]

The political parties in Nepal took birth in the Indian soil just after latter's independence. The Nepali Congress and the Communist Party of Nepal were originated in India. Though some political groups had formed by the Nepalese who were turning in exile in India during the course of Indian National Movement, Nepali Congress was first to take the shape of a political party followed by the Communist party of Nepal.

The 1950 political change in Nepal gave opportunity to the political parties to participate in the political process and work towards the establishment of a democratic political system in the country.[4] They were also required to establish their social base in the country. The political change in the country lead to the emergence of new political groups and parties but none could emerge to the expectations of the people of Nepal. The political parties soon entered into factional politics and leadership conflicts, with the result that it gave opportunity for the consolidation of traditional political forces. The feudal nature of Nepali state and backward and rigid social conditions also proved to be non-conducive to the emergence of political parties with a strong social base.

There was a brief interlude of 18 months in February 1959 when Nepali Congress got opportunity to rule the country under a democratic Political order. But with the abrogation of the parliamentary democracy in December 1960 this opportunity was lost. The Panchayat system that came into operation in 1962 had an essentially non-political party character. No organized political activities were allowed and all the political parties were declared illegal. Thus, the political parties got only a decade's time to operate. It was indeed a formative stage when political parties not only had to create their organizational base but also to fight with the reactionary social and political forces. When the time came to operate under a full-fledged democratic system they were dislodged unnoticed. After 1962 political parties were not allowed to operate till 1990 when the panchayat system was abrogated. This long absence of political parties from the active politics caused erosion of their social and political base. The individual political leaders of different political parties though continued to oppose the panchayat system; the growth of a party system was seriously injured after the establishment of panchayat system.

In a way political parties got opportunity to function in a democratic system only after 1990. But their long absence from the political scenario has clearly reflected in their working, role and attitude. It seems that the political parties have not been able to come out of the hangovers of the past. The three general elections in the post-1990 phase clearly indicate that none of the political parties are in a position to gain majority in the elections, except Nepali Congress with a razor thin majority. Political parties are sharply divided internally. But interestingly the internal factions in the political parties are not on ideological grounds. They are based on the conflict for leadership or have been personalised.[5] The Nepali Congress, after the death of B.P. Koirala adopted a formula of collective leadership. But it seems that it did not work well and gave rise to leadership clashes. These clashes became more expressive after 1990 when the party got opportunity to come into power. Thus the party was infected with serious horizontal leadership conflicts. After 1995 when the second rank leadership of the party got opportunity to head the government, as the top leadership was sharply divided, the vertical leadership conflicts also began to surface. The party leadership has not shown resilience and adopted a compromising attitude for their own interest.[6] This ultimately led to a split in the Nepali Congress. Thus the assumption that the party had sufficient resilience and capability to resolve its internal disputes got eroded.

The UML got divided in 1997. The National Democratic Party had already divided into two and the Sadbhavana Party also faced similar challenges. All these splits had emanated out of leadership conflicts. As a result of these conflicts political parties lacked the necessary strength and capability to take part in democratic process, take up developmental issues and work for the realization of popular needs and aspirations.

The ideological content of political parties has remained quite week and ambiguous.[7] The Nepali Congress since its inception adhered to the ideology of democratic socialism. The communists were divided into liberal communism, Marxists and the ultra leftists. The National Democratic parties have been labeled as supporters of panchayat era. But in the post-1990 period none of the political parties have given any impression of their ideological commitment. They have believed in reality in the politics of opportunism.

Political parties are more oriented towards seeking power than building their own base. They have been compromising with their ideological background and commitments in order to seek power. Thus, Nepali Congress agreed to form coalition government with NDP or hard core communists while UML formed coalition with NDP. It is true that seeking power has to be the ultimate goal of a political party. But they are expected to do it by following certain norms and principles and on their own basis. The objective to seek power should be based for a well defined goal and while doing so the political parties are expected not to compromise with their commitments. But it seems that in Nepal political parties have failed largely in observing these norms of democracy. It has weakened the creditability of political parties, it has lead to the deterioration in their social base and it has weakened the democratic process.

Political parties are faced with a highly complex situation in Nepal. Their long absence from active politics eroded their social and organizational base. On the other hand, after 1990 they became impatient to seek power and positions. It was obvious that political parties utterly failed in bearing their responsibilities in a democratic system. The governmental instability, negligence to developmental issues, rise in popular discontent, corruption, etc., were largely attributed to the functioning of political parties. Although it would be wrong to conclude that political parties alone were responsible for the complications in the post-1990 Nepali politics, it can be said that political parties failed in carrying their own responsibility properly and it resultantly paved way for the strengthening of forces that proved to be more disastrous to democracy in Nepal in the subsequent years.

It would be interesting to note that none of the political parties have been able to democratize themselves internally. The caste and class character of the party leadership is similar and unchanged in the case of almost all the major political parties. The party leadership still belongs to the high caste Brahmin-Chettri–Newar castes, which have been traditionally enjoying high political and economic status due to their caste status. Even the leftist and revolutionary parties have not been exception to this trend. The party leadership is generally identified with the hill culture. It is for these reasons that it is not difficult to find out the allegiance of party leaders to monarchy.

The intra-party conflicts have been a remarkable feature of Nepali party system. The competitive politics is a healthy indication of a party system. But it should be based on certain principles of democracy. But in Nepal intra-party conflicts are mainly due to struggle for power, personalized politics, and personal abuses.

The Panchayat elite had a vested interest in continuing with the traditional bases of power and authority as they were dependent on those caste and class categories which were pillars of power traditionally. But the political parties failed after 1990 in broadening the socio-economic bases of power and authority. There was a need to bring up a social transformation in the country so that the dominance of the high caste people in the politico-administrative structures could be reduced and the framework is broadened to depressed sections and regions of the country. It seems that the political parties missed this opportunity due to political instability and struggle for power. But the political parties also had a vested interest in the continuation of the traditional structures of power because the party leadership also belonged to those groups and their dominance over political parties would have continued with the continuation of the upper caste, upper class and hill dominance over the politico-administrative structures.

In this respect it can be said that the political parties have lacked the necessary dynamism and far sight.

Monarchy Vis-a-Vis Democracy

It is interesting to recall here that in the post-1950 political transition in Nepal it was monarchy who was assigned the responsibility to carry the project of installation of democracy in the country. The newly emerged democratic forces were to share power with the monarchy and work for the introduction of democracy. It was however, not easy for the democratic forces to operate in a feudal social order and highly backward economic conditions. The political parties apart from the prevailing adverse socio-economic conditions suffered from their own shortcomings and in capabilities. It gave an edge to the monarchy over democratic forces. The monarchy already had a support base in the form of traditional forces that were trying to realign around the king. The socio-economic conditions too were supportive to monarchy.

King Tribhuwan was obliged to democratic forces as well as to India for the restoration of its powers. Moreover, he had spent most of his life silently under the clinches of the Rana rule. So he was not that ambitious politically. But as an ambitious young monarch when Mahendra took reigns of power in 1955, dynamics of power began to take a turn in Nepal. King Mahendra took advantage of the prevailing conditions to promote his political interest. He raised a propaganda that the political parties were incapable in carrying the cause of democracy and that western democracy was not suitable to Nepali conditions. King Mahendra though saw installation of democracy in Nepal during 1959-60, he could not contain his own political interest and ambitions. He dislodged the parliamentary democracy and he took powers. King Mahendra's action changed the course of democracy in the country. It is clear that in the tug of war between traditional and modern political forces the traditional forces emerged victorious and the king emerged as the main custodian of the traditional forces. The monarchy also played the role of a modernizing agent.[8] Monarchy also projected itself as an integrative force in the Nepalese society and the custodian of Nepali culture and traditions.[9]

King Mahendra envisaged a system that ensured his supreme political authority and kept at bay his main political competitors; the political parties. It can be said the monarchy has been the major stumbling block to democracy. It is true that the political parties too had many weaknesses for which they did not succeeded in promoting democracy. But it was monarchy which created conditions for the ineffectiveness of political parties.

It may again be stressed here that the socio-cultural context remained in favour of the institution of monarchy. The feudal class had their vested interest in aligning with the king. It was obvious that the position of the king was strengthened. The monarchy remained a major political force.[10]

If we look back to the world history there are examples where a complete transfer from monarchic authoritarian to democratic forces had taken place. In some countries such institutions survive even today under the umbrella of strong democratic traditions. But there are examples where there was a comeback of the authoritarian forces into politics after a certain gap. It has indeed depended on the capability of the democratic forces, popular perception and consciousness, prevailing socio-cultural and economic milieu, the civil society and soon. In Nepal there has been a democratic fervour in the country. But the societal conditions have not been supportive to it. Therefore, it has not been possible to lay a strong foundation of democracy in the country. Monarchy has succeeded in creating a political space for itself.

Whenever an assertive king has taken over to reigns of power he has succeeded in utilizing this political space for his direct entry to power. It is because of the strong religio-cultural foundation of monarchy and the impact of past traditions on the Nepalese political culture that monarchy has always emerged as the grantor of democracy. The democratic institutions and actors have looked towards monarchy as their ultimate source of power and a friend, philosopher and guide. The democratic forces have not been able to come out of these psychological barriers. It has naturally hampered the growth of democracy as an independent political philosophy and on the contrary, the monarchy was looked as the saviour of Nepalese people, state and democracy.

Even after the 1990 political change monarchy remained an important pillar of Nepali politics. Nepal though opted for a constitutional monarchy the institutions, beliefs and values that would provide strength to monarchy continued. Nepal was again declared a Hindu state in the 1990 constitution. The socio-economic structures that had traditionally been supportive to the monarchy more or less continued. The king was still regarded as a major integrative force. King's prestige and role as a religio-cultural institution of high order continued. Thus, though the political change in Nepal reduced the political role of the monarchy his social and religio-cultural role continued as earlier. The declining role of monarchy would have been possible had the political behaviour and political culture gone a change in Nepal, had the democratic forces gained self-confidence and mutual trust and had they worked for the strengthening and stabilization of democratic institutions. Unfortunately this did not happen and as a result monarchy retained its political significance in different ways.

The way democratic forces acted during the decade of 90's it certainly weakened the democratic process but King Birendra did not try to play any assertive role. However, after his sad demise when an ambitious king Gyanendra took over the thrown he began to assert politically. The prevailing political situation marked by governmental instability, insurgency, inter-party and intra-party clashes, etc., went in favour of king Gyanendra's political assertion. He began with appointing a government of his choice and than taking over all powers in his hands in February 2005.[11] With the April, 2006 movement again a situation have arrived where monarchy is being reduced politically. To what extent this process will go only the new constitution of Nepal will be able to indicate.

It can be said that the process of democratization in Nepal after 1950 has been a history of tug of war between the political parties and the monarchy. No doubt monarchy has proved to be a stumbling block to democracy in the country. It is difficult to state with any certainty how much Nepalese political parties have learned from history. But it can be said that the future of democracy will remain bleak in Nepal so long the institution of monarchy continues. Because one can observe that there has not been any perceptional and attitudinal change in monarchy. Secondly, one is also reminded of the fact that it is not only a question of monarchy it is a question of the class that it represents, the philosophy that it represents and the power orientation that it represents. This particular class is yet to be transformed and it still looks towards monarchy for its sustenance. This feudal royal clique which has been at the core of Nepal's failure in social upliftment and democratic degeneration cannot be transformed unless the political role of monarchy is not totally abandoned.

Nepali Political Culture and Democracy

Political culture is the opinion hold by people in a society about their political institutions, political actors, perception, role and behaviour.[12] The political culture of a country is shaped by the political values and behaviours that are installed in its people as a process of their socialization. The political culture of a society changes slowly in a long-term process.[13]

Our purpose here is not to enter into any detailed commentaries on the political culture in Nepal, but just to understand to what extent the political culture of Nepal has been conducive to democracy and to what extent it has been possible to inculcate a democratic political culture in the country in the process of its transition to a democratic political order.

Nepal was ruled for a long time under a highly centralized, authoritarian and personalized political system of the Shah Kings and the Rana Prime Ministers. The rulers of Nepal forged dependent relationship in the society in which the rulers were the patron and the masses as clients. Allegiance to the ruler was a precondition for entering into the power structure. However, for any such allegiance it was necessary that the person belongs to higher castes and hill culture. It gave way to a system of patronage. The authoritarian feudal mentality of the Shah and the Rana rulers did not allow any short of dissent or opposition. It was considered to be the breach of faith and sever punishment was prescribed for it. As a result, people lacked self-confidence, openness, security and consciousness. People remained suppressed and under the obsequious attendance of the rulers. The Nepali rulers did not distinguish between political, social and personal relations.[14] It helped them establishing their absolute possession of the people and resources. The king was identified with the state.[15]

Thus the Nepali Political traditions were characterized by authoritarianism, absolutism, dependency, people's obligations to authority, social relations based on power hierarchy and patron-client relations.[16]

Nepal's transition to democratization and political change in the post-1950 period has been marked by a conflict between traditional cultural norms and the dynamics of multiparty democracy. The continuation of the traditional political elite and its assertion over politics has resulted in contradictions in Nepali society and politics. The modern political forces have not been able to inculcate liberal democratic values in the society due to these contradictions. The notions of authoritarianism, personalized politics, lack of self-confidence, feudalistic orientation allegiance to power, impatience, exclusiveness, lack of consensus as fundamental national issues personalized advantages, etc., became the major characteristics of the post-1950 Nepali politics.

The reassertion of authoritarian-feudal forces in politics weakened the democratic forces. It is true that the authoritarian forces could not eliminate the thrust of democracy that had been aroused in the country. The democratic forces continued their struggle in one form or the other. But the democratic transformation that was expected after 1950 was not realized. Therefore, the political norms, values and political behaviour remained the same. In a way it got complicated because of the persistence of traditional forces and the struggle of the modern democratic forces. Actually, the inculcation of a democratic political culture requires a strong foundation of democratic institutions and governance and its growth in a long-term. But it did not happen in Nepal as in the decade of 1950's the experiment on democracy did not bear fruits. There was a brief interlude of democracy in 1959-60 and after 1960 the democratic governance was over powered by the authoritarian rule of monarchy under the garb of panchayat system. The ruling elite of Nepal followed an exclusionist approach instead of broadening the politico administrative structures. This obviously narrowed the bases of politics in Nepal.[17]

The transformation to a democratic system after the 1990 movement was a significant development in Nepal. The political change in Nepal called for a change in the political behaviour and political culture. However, there does not appear to be sufficient evidence to show that the political culture has undergone a change in Nepal. There are still problems of social transformation and broadening of the political system. The ideology does not play a major role in politics. The feudal elite continue to play its role in politics. The participatory approach to politics is weak. It can be said that despite installation of democracy in the country, the evolution of democratic political culture still appears to be a distant dream. The basic contours of Nepali politics are not much changed.

Concluding Observations

It can be concluded here that Nepal has lacked a conducive political background for the successful working of democracy. The democratic institutions have been weak, facing demolition and erosion. It has not been possible to sustain democracy. The political parties, which were suppose to be the main actors in the institutionalization of democracy could not play their role. It is true that the political parties fought again and again for the restoration of democracy but they were faced with many shot comings. The hangover of the past loomed large in their political actions, behaviour and role. The political culture of Nepal remained almost unchanged not conducive to the working of democratic institutions.

The traditional political forces represented by monarchy proved to be a stumbling block to democracy. Not only that the traditional elite made sustenance of democratic institutions difficult but democracy was overpowered by them. It seems that despite installation of democracy a sufficiently conducive environment for the sustenance and growth of democracy could not match it. Therefore, creating democratic structures itself is not sufficient it is equally important in what conditions these institutions have to be work.

REFERENCES

1. See for details, B.C. Upreti, *Nepali Congress, A Study of Party's Performance in 1991 General Elections and Aftermath,* Nirala Publications, New Delhi, 1993.
2. See, B.C. Upreti, "Nepal's Relations with India during the Communist Regime", *Journal of International Relations* (Dhaka), Vol. 5, Nos 1 & 2, July–June, 1997-98: 53–68.
3. Robert Michels, *Political Parties: A Sociological Study of the Oligarchical Tendencies of Modern Democracy,* New York, 1959. John W. Derry, Political Parties, Macmillan, New York, 1968.
4. For a study of emergence of political parties in Nepal see, Krishna Hatchethu, *Party Building in Nepal, Organisation, Leadership and People,* Mandola Book Point, Kathmandu, 2002.
5. For a case study in this regard see, B.C. Upreti, "Intra-Party Cleavages within Nepali Congress: A Study in the context of 1994 Kathmandu By Election", *South Asian Studies,* Vols. 31, 31 Nos. 1 & 2, January–December, 1996: 13–36.
6. Lok Raj Baral, *et al., Leadership in Nepal,* Adroit Publishers, Delhi, 2001: 41.
7. N. 6: 33.
8. See, Louis D. Hayes, "The Monarchy and Modernization in Nepal", *Asian Survey,* Vol. XV, No. 7, July 1975.
9. B.C. Upreti, "Monarchy and Nation Building in Nepal" in S.K. Chaube (ed.), *The Himalayas, Profile of Modernization and Adaption,* Sterling Publications, New Delhi, 1985: 185–194.
10. See, Rishikesh Shaha, *Three Decades and Two Kings, 1960-90,* Sterling Publishers, Delhi 1990: 78–92.
11. B.C. Upreti, "Will Monarchy Survive", in *Seminar* (546), April 2005, 15-17.
12. See for theoretical postulates, Gabriel Almond & Sidney Verba (eds), *The Civic Culture: Political Attitudes and Democracy in Five Nations,*

Princeton, 1963; Almond & Verba (eds.), The Civic Culture Revisited, Boston, 1980.

13. N. 12, Introduction. Also see, Larry Diamond (ed.), *Political Culture and Democracy in Developing Countries*, Boulder, 1993.
14. Ole Borre, Sushil R. Pandey and Chitra K. Tiwari, *Nepali Political Behaviour*, Sterling Publisher, Delhi, 1993.
15. Richard Burghaut, *The Conditions of Listening, Essays on Religion, History and Politics in South Asia*, Oxford University Press, Delhi, 1996: 226–260.
16. Ole Borre N. 14: 145–146.
17. Mahendra Lawati, *Towards a Democratic Nepal*, Sage Publications, New Delhi, 2005: 87–112.

8
Restoration of Democracy

The democratic governance was fast loosing grounds in Nepal with frequent governmental changes leading to Political instability, misgovernance and conflicts. The Maoist insurgency was yet another important factor adding to political instability and chaos in the country. The final blow to the democracy arrived with the brutal murder of King Birendra along with his whole family on June 1, 2001. It was not merely the murder of a king but it also put an end to the constitutional monarchy that was gradually and with great difficulties taking roots in the country. It was not immediately realized that King Birendra's sad demise was also a serious blow to democracy in Nepal. Only the later developments proved it.

The constitutional and political apparatus that came into fore in 1990 in Nepal needed sometime for its stabilization and strengthening. It was a complex issue in the context of Nepali political conditions. There were doubts wheatear the political parties would succeed in democratic stability and good governance. There were also apprehensions whether the monarchy would accept the role of a constitutional head. But King Birendra had tried to act in accordance to the norms of a constitutional monarchy. This process, however, stopped with his demise and it appears that the new king had an entirely different political approach.

In the post-Birendra period four types of forces became prominent in Nepal's politics. King Gyanendra who was looking for an active political role; the political parties, which despite their fragmentation and conflicts wanted continuation of the multi-party democracy; the Maoists who were struggling for restructuring the state and society in which monarchy would not have any place and the royal armed forces that had also become an important political force due to their deployment to contain the emergency. The armed forces were loyal to the king. The monarchy also had a support base in the bureaucracy, the old nobility and feudalistic sections of the society and above all members of the royalty who also wanted king to be active in politics. All these factors made an ambitious king Gyanendra impatient to over rule the democracy.

The pro-democracy forces though active to fight against the anti-democratic activities of the king were divided. King Gyanendra tried his best to keep the political parties fragmented and the political parties and the Maoists at a bay. It was quite clear that monarchy's ascendance to power could be challenged only with the political parties and the Maoists coming together. This happened towards the end of 2005 and consequently a new struggle for democracy began. The story was not different from that of late eighties when communist forces came together and made a joint front with the Nepali Congress to over throw the Panchayat rule. Similarly, the understanding between seven political parties and the Maoists forced the king to reinstate democracy in the country. History has been repeating itself again and again in Nepal. One can only hope that this becomes the last struggle for democracy in the country.

This chapter is devoted to the circumstances leading to monarchy's direct rule and the restoration of democracy, and the post-conflict transformation in Nepal that has to set a stage for the sustenance of democracy in the country.

Dissolution of the Parliament

The political situation was not peaceful in Nepal after declaring emergency on 26 November, 2001. The royal army was fighting to contain insurgency, while the Maoist forces were retaliating in a big way. The army was under the control of the king and it was not prepared to follow the instructions of the government. There were serious pulls and pressures within the Nepali Congress Party. Above all the king was not prepared to tolerate political parties and the parliamentary government. All these factors made it difficult for Deuba to run the government. On 22 May, 2002 Sher Bahadur Deuba resigned and he recommended for the dissolution of the parliament. King Gyanendra readily accepted the recommendation. It was decided that elections for a new House of Representatives would be held in 6 months time. Is the decision for the dissolution of the house was taken by the PM and his cabinet? Did his party instruct Dueba? Or that it was the king who instigated him? It is true that Nepal was passing through a difficult phase after the failure of peace talks and the consequent deployment of armed forces against the Maoists. But where would have it been helpful in meeting the challengers? It seems that there was no need to dissolve the parliament. It only added to political instability. It is also believed that the Prime Minister might have come under the pressure of the ambitious king to dissolve the house.[1] It should be noted here that the dissolution of the House of Representatives could have proved to be a gateway to king's rise to power.

Internal Developments in NC

The internal developments within the Nepali Congress were not less responsible for the political developments that took place in the middle of 2002. G.P. Koirala resigned from the Prime Ministership and Sher Bahadur Deuba was made Prime Minister on 2001. After sometimes pressure was being mounted on Deuba by the Koirala group. The Koirala group was not happy with Deuba's decision to dissolve the house. As a strong reaction to these developments Sher Bahadur Deuba was suspended from the party for three years on 26 May, 2002. The Party was heading towards a split because of a non-compromising attitude of its leaders. On 16 June, 2002 Sher Bahadur Deuba faction of Nepali Congress declared formation of a new political party called Nepali Congress (Democratic). The split within Nepali Congress took place at a time when the democracy was at a stake in the country. Interestingly neither the Nepali Congress party remained united nor could Deuba secure his government by forming a new party. It not only shows dethroning of his government but also weakened the democratic forces.

Prime Minister Deuba failed in holding elections. Actually the cabinet took a decision that in the prevailing situation in the country it was not possible to hold the elections. The Maoists had already threatened to disrupt the elections. It was suggested to postpone the general elections till March 2003 and after that elections could be held in different phases. But King Gyanendra conceived it as an incompetence of the government. Deuba was sacked on 4th October and king took back all executive powers. It was indeed the first submission of the king towards the consolidation of his powers and against the continuation of parliamentary democracy.[2]

Political Instability and Uncertainty Again

King Gyanendra's action against the elected government and his assuming a direct role in politics did not help resolving the problems. In fact, apart from the continuation of governmental instability, there was a general deterioration in the political situation as King's action had agitated the political parties.

On 12 October, 2002 Lokendra Bahadur Chand was nominated Prime Minister by the king. Chand a leader of the National Democratic Party had been a trusted person of the monarchy during the panchayat era. King Gyanendra wanted an active political role and more than that he wanted to show to the countrymen that he has proved more effective in conflict resolution in comparison to the elected government. This would have also given him legitimacy and would have justified his action. So he gave top priority to the resolution of the Maoist problem. On 29 January, 2003 the government and the Maoists announced a ceasefire. The first round of formal talks between the government and the Maoists took place on 24 April, 2003. Prime Minister Thapa had to resign on 30 May and Surya Bahadur Chand another trusted leader of the Panchayat era was appointed new Prime Minister. Thapa also followed talks with the Maoists. Third round of talks was held between the Maoists and the government nominated negotiation team on 11 August, 2003 in Dang. Maoists stuck to their earlier demands while government was not prepared to accept any of them. It was obvious that the negotiations failed and the Maoists declared withdrawal of ceasefire on 26 August. The Maoists once again took resort to violence. The government lacked any concrete proposal for the peace negotiations. Moreover, there was distrust on both sides against each other.

Towards the beginning of 2004 pressure began to mount on Surya Bahadur Thapa from within the Party to quit the government. He was threatened that he would be expelled from the membership of the party. Thapa resigned on 7 May, 2004. This brought yet another governmental change. This time Deuba was nominated as Prime Minister of Nepal, the same person whom king Gyanendra had expelled as Prime Minister; a person who had the claim of being people's representative. Deuba accepted it and became Prime Minister on July 4, 2004. There was no ideology no commitment and no principles of politics. It was a power game indeed. Some other political parties like National Jan Morcha, UML, etc., also joined the government. King played politics of divide and rule. Actually king was under pressure from the international community to take steps towards the restoration of multi-party democracy. By appointing Deuba as the Prime Minister he wanted to give this impression that he had conceded to the need for the restoration of democracy in the country. Surprisingly the international community seemed satisfactory with the steps taken by the king, while the later was looking forward for the establishment of his despotic rule in the country.

The Royal Cup

In a highly surprising way king Gyanendra dismissed the Sher Bahadur Deuba government on 1 February, 2005 and declared a state of emergency in the country. In his announcement king Gyanendra said that he will himself assume all powers and rule the country directly as Chairman of the council of ministers for a period of three years.[3] The King took advantage of the constitutional provisions under Article 19 which provide for emergency powers to the King. However, Gyanendra's action was uncalled for as there was no such urgency for declaring emergency in the country. The kind of situation prevailed in the country had continued for last many years and there was nothing extra ordinary. Secondly, the way king acted was beyond the spirit of the constitution.[4] It was not clear as what was the justification behind announcing king's direct rule for three years? It was clear that the king was highly ambitious. But no one would have thought of such a drastic and early action by king Gyanendra. The royal Nepali army assisted the king in implementing his political motives.[5]

King Gyanendra's assumption of powers followed a series of actions against his political adversaries. Main political leaders were house arrested or detained or placed in jails. All kinds of communications such as media, radio and telecommunication were brought under control. Media persons, intellectuals and other persons of civil society who were considered to be the supporters of democracy were also arrested or they were compelled not to move outside their city or district. It is clear that King Gyanendra defied the 1990 constitution and democracy and imposed his personal despotism in the country.

Return to Panchayat Era

King Gyanendra wanted to create a support base, which would strengthen his despotic rule and at the same time dawn the democratic forces. The royal army was already supporting him. What he now needed to create was a political support base. For this purpose he decided to take support of the old guards of the panchayat era. On 2 February king announced a 10 member council of ministers. On 14 February he appointed Tulsi Giri and Kirti Nidhi Bisht as Vice-Chairman of the Council of Ministers. King brought back those leaders of the panchayat era who had been out of active politics since long. But they had been strong supporters of the monarchy. Thus king tried to return to panchayat era.[6]

The Council of Ministers in its first meeting announced a 21-point programme. A Corruption Control Royal Commission was also formed to look in to cases of corruption. It was an important instrument to take in to task all the political adversaries and opponents. In order to establish its control over the district administration the king appointed Zonal Commissioners in all the 14 administrative zones and development regions, as it was during the panchayat system. King tried to consolidate his powers with the help of royal army and the panchayat era political leadership. In the middle of the year he announced withdrawal of the emergency. But control over media, communication etc., continued. Actually, it was done just to satisfy the international community, which was pressurizing the king to return to multi-party democracy. The king continued with its absolute control over state power.

King Gyanendra also sought support from the international community in the name of controlling the Maoist insurgency. India, USA, UK and other though not happy with the action of king Gyanendra continued to support him over the issue of armed action against the Maoists. Thus there was a duality in the perception of these powers. It was tried to make arms assistance conditional but these countries did not stuck to these pre-conditions. Nepal also sought support from China, Pakistan, Russia, etc.

Seven Parties Political Alliance

The king adopted a confrontationist attitude and was not prepared to negotiate with the political parties or the Maoists. He was critical of the political parties and blamed them for not taking the Maoists problem seriously. The king also blamed them for misgovernance, corruption and weakening the process of national integration.

King's actions against the leaders of various political parties further pull them apart. King's take over of political powers had already created a hiatus between the Monarchy and the political parties. The disgusted political parties began to search for a united struggle against the king's take over. In May 2005 seven political parties including NC, UML, NC(D), etc., agreed to form an alliance to fight against the despotic rule of the king. The seven party alliance agreed on a 6-point programme that included restoration of the House of Representatives and the 1990 constitution, management of conflict, progressive movement for the restoration of democracy on the basis of 1990 constitution, adherence to multi-party democracy and elections for a Constituent Assembly.[7]

The seven party alliances gave top priority to the restoration of the House of Representatives. It is, however, doubtful if this would have resolved the crisis. Once the House was restored it could bring to the forefront yet another crisis of government formation. The NC had already undergone a split than this would not have been acceptable to the Maoists unless until they were fully convinced that this process would lead to the formation of Constituent Assembly ultimately. Nevertheless, the seven party alliances was the first major attempt of the political parties against the royal take over. It also paved a way for the polarization of democratic forces. It also gave a positive message to the civil society. On the whole it was a significant development and generated new hopes among the democratic forces.

The Maoist Ceasefire

The Maoist declared a three month unilateral ceasefire to be effective from September 2005. The ceasefire was further extended for a month in December 2005. The government refused to respond to the ceasefire arguing that Maoists were not serious to conflict resolution but were seeking opportunity to consolidate themselves. It was apparent that the government was not prepared to enter into any negotiations with the Maoists. It was also clear that the Maoists too were not expecting any positive response from the king. The Maoists knew that king Gyanendra did not bear a positive attitude towards them. The Maoists too were highly critical of king's take over and they now believed that the democracy should be restored. The political parties too wanted to fight for the restoration of democracy. They were gradually accepting the need for a constituent assembly. On the other hand, Maoist leaders had opined to cooperate with the political parties against the royal take over. The Maoists had in a way succeeded in distancing political parties from the king. It is in this perspective probably that the Maoist ceasefire may be understood. The Maoist ceasefire helped in building confidence among the political parties as well as the civil society regarding their motives. The Maoists also succeeded in giving a message to the international community as well, that they also believe in conflict resolution and peace building.

It is a fact that the king was playing the terrorist card in order to seek cooperation and arms assistance from the international community. By declaring unilateral ceasefire Maoists tried to isolate the king and create an adverse position from him.

Though the Maoist ceasefire did not bear any results in a formal way as far as the question of conflict resolution was concerned it was an important development for three broad reasons. The Maoists utilized this time in consolidating their organizational base and streamlined their activities and programmes; it gave a positive message to international community and the civil society in Nepal; it brought the Maoists and the political parties nearer and isolated the king.

Understanding Between Maoists and Political Parties

The polarization of pro-democratic forces against the despotic rule of the king took a concrete shape towards the end of year 2005. In the middle of November, 2005 leaders of the seven party alliance started consultations for a collaboration with the Maoists.[8] The leaders of NC, UML, NC(D) came to New Delhi for consultations with the Indian Political leaders. Three top Maoist leaders: Pushp Kamal Dahal, Babu Ram Bhattarai and Krishna Bahadur Mahar also said to had visited New Delhi for consultations with the Indian leaders and the Nepali political leaders who had visited New Delhi at that time. These consultations proved to be important for an understanding between the Maoists and the seven party's alliance. On 17 November the groups agreed on a 12-point understanding. It emphasized re-structuring of the state for the establishment of absolute democracy in the country. There was an understanding to do away with the constitutional monarchy.[9] The 12 points were as following:

1. To establish absolute democracy by abandoning autocratic monarchic rule, there by creating an atmosphere for long-term peace and stability.
2. Restoration of the House of Representatives, form an all party government and work towards holding elections for a Constituent Assembly.
3. Bringing an end to armed conflict through a dialogue and seek international mediation for this purpose.
4. Expressing commitment to democratic norms, and values and complete faith on multi-party democracy, civil liberties, human rights, rule of law and the fundamental rights.
5. The CPN (Maoist) expressed its commitment to create a congenial environment for the installation of democracy by allowing political activists of various political parties to return to their earlier positions, who had been displaced during insurgency.
6. The CPN (Maoist) expressed its commitment not to repeat past mistakes.
7. The seven parties alliance expressed commitment not to repeat past mistakes, while in government.
8. Respect to the norms and values of human rights and press freedom and move ahead accordingly.
9. Boycott of the forthcoming municipal elections as they were announced by the king with attractive motives.
10. Commitment to protect the independence, sovereignty, geographical integrity of the country and national unity. Maintenance of peaceful relations with all countries based on the principle of peaceful co-existence and good neighbourly relations with the neighbouring countries.
11. Call to civil society, professional organizations, diverse communities and regions, intellectuals and the media to participate in the peaceful movement to be launched on the basis of understanding between the political parties and the Maoists.
12. To settle any problem emerging between the two through peaceful dialogue at the concerned level or at the leadership level.

The Maoist–seven party alliance understanding was an important development and a much needed step to be taken by both. However, doubts were also raised regarding sincerity of Maoists and the workability of the alliance. The U.S. Ambassador to Nepal J.F. Moriarty warned political parties not to enter into any collaboration with the Maoists.[10]

The Civic Polls

In October, 2005 the Nepali Government decided to hold elections for the 57 municipalities in February 2006 and general elections in 2008. The seven party alliance strongly reacted against the decision as the elections would be held under an undemocratic environment. It also decided to boycott the municipal elections. The Maoists also declared to boycott the elections. However, the king was determined to hold the elections. It seems that the king was looking for gaining people's faith and legitimacy. It was also an effort to convey that monarchy was concerned about representative governance. The elections would also act as a test case for future course of action towards political liberalization. However, the civil polls were a complete fiasco. It is true that neither Maoists nor political parties could prevent king Gyanendra to hold elections of municipalities, it was clear that the people did not trust the king. Out of 75 districts elections were held in 28 districts. The voting turn out was only 21 per cent, which was lowest in the history of elections in Nepal. At most of the places the election remained uncontested. The king was badly exposed in these elections. It became clear that he lacked credibility. The people did not trust the king that he was willing to restore democracy. The United States termed these elections a hollow attempt by the king to legitimize power.[11]

The lack of public support to the king encouraged the democratic forces.

Movement to Restore Democracy

In March, 2006, it was decided to launch a movement for the restoration of democracy. The movement that was finally initiated in April against the direct rule of the king received widespread support from all walks of the civil society. It was clear that the monarchy had lost popular faith. It was for the first time that the monarchy was denounced by the political parties and the people. The movement launched by the seven party political alliance had full backing of Maoists. The king tried his best to curb the movement. Curfew was imposed in Kathmandu. But it could not prevent people from organizing widespread demonstrations against the king. The crackdown over people by the Government further agitated the people. The king was abused and denounced like a common man.[12] On 21 April, 2006 Kathmandu saw most wide spread and furious mass uprising in its history of last 237 years.[13] It appeared that the king was badly exposed and there was a strong internal pressure on him. King's policy of suppression was not fruit bearing. King also came under strong external pressure and he had to agree to step down.

India's Mediation

At a time when a strong anti-king movement was brewing in Nepal, Government of India decided to send a senior political leader Karan Singh to Nepal to pursue the king for a solution to the crisis. India's concern was that a peaceful political solution of the problem was an urgent requirement.[14] India's message for the king of Nepal was that "if he wishes to salvage the situation he should handover power to a representative of SPA."[15] Karan's visit to Kathmandu naturally aroused lot of excitement and speculations. He being a member of a royal family having connections with the royalty in Nepal was interpreted in one way while his coming to Nepal at a time of deep political crisis as a representative of the Prime Minister of India was interpreted in many other ways. Karan Singh met the king, leaders of political parties, members of civil society, etc. He made it clear that India would not like to involve in the internal affairs of Nepal; and that he was not there to advice the Nepalese but to articulate India's concern in Nepal.[16] There is no doubt that Karan Singh prepared a strong ground for the restoration of democracy. Communist leader Sita Ram Yechury followed his visit to Nepal. The Indian foreign secretary, army chief and other leaders also played a role. India no doubt played a balancing act and helped bringing normalcy in Nepal.[17] But India's role, as usual, was not above controversy. There are two aspects one is that many people and groups in Nepal and elsewhere have always misperceived India mediation, role etc. With whatever best intentions India would have acted, controversies are bound to erupt. Secondly, India did give such impressions which were interpreted as Indian favour to monarchy. For instance Karan Singh's nomination for mediation was bound to raise controversy due to his very identity as a member of a royal family. There was lack of clarity as well, on the part of India. There were contradictory statements that created doubts and misgivings. It seems that India could not articulate its diplomatic postures the way it should have been. India also gave the impression as if it was favouring a role for the monarchy in the new set up.[18] India could have avoided these controversial issues. Why did India decide to mediate? There have been many opinions in this regard. One opinion is that India wanted to save the monarchy because India thought that her security would be in danger with the abolition of monarchy in Nepal. Another opinion was that India thought that Maoists would succeed in getting a political space.

It is true that India was concerned about the deteriorating political situation in Nepal. India's concerns were three:

(i) As a democratic and secular state India was concerned to the restoration of democracy in that country. India thought that a first step towards that direction could be handing over power to the democratic forces through restoration of House of Representatives. The democratic forces and the Maoists could decide the future course after that.

(ii) Because of a close neighbour having strategically important, India was concerned about security and stability in the Himalayan region. Due to the open border between the two countries, interactions between Nepali insurgents and extremists group in Nepal, etc., security risks were high for India as well.

(iii) The large scale Nepali migration to the bordering region of India was an issue of vital concern. The continuation of violence, instability and royal despotism would have further increased cross border migration.

Restoration of the Parliament

King Gyanendra could not resist the pressure of democratic forces and after 18 days agitation declared to restore the 1999 House of Representatives and handover power to the leader of the seven party's alliance. In his announcement the king said:

"…. The ideals of democracy can be realized only through the active participation of political parties. In keeping with the traditions of the Shah Dynasty to reign in accordance with the

popular will in greater interest of the nation and the people and our unflinching commitment towards constitutional Monarchy and multiparty democracy, we through this proclamation, affirm that the executive power of the kingdom of Nepal, which was in our safe keeping, shall from this day, be returned to the people and be exercised in accordance with Article 35 of the constitution of the kingdom of Nepal ..... 1990."[19]

What compelled the king to withdraw? King Gyanendra had tried to defuse the democratic forces and also to keep political parties and Maoists apart. But now the two had come closer. It was not possible to withstand their pressure for long. King was also under the pressure of the international community. India had already suggested to the king to restore the parliament. There were clear indications that the monarchy was loosing its respect and importance and that the people were becoming highly critical of king Gyanendra's role. It is also said that dissatisfaction was gradually brewing up among the armed forces, while king was dependent on the support of the armed forces.

The seven party political alliance welcomed king's declaration to restore the 1999 parliament. The Maoists did not appreciate it as they believed that it would delay Nepal's heading towards the goal of elections for the Constituent Assembly. They alleged that the seven party's alliance was betraying the people's movement.[20] However, later on, they agreed to the situation. The SPA elected G.P. Koirala of NC as its leader. Madhav Nepal leader of UML declared that "the announcement of Constituent Assembly elections will be the main agenda of the reinstated parliament."[21]

The Parliament was reconvened on 28 April. The speaker of the House of Representatives Taranath Bhatt was forced to resign for his controversial role during the king's rule.[22] The Deputy Speaker proposed on behalf of Prime Minister G.P. Koirala who was ill, that "it is the people who have brought this change and we have to live up to the expectations."[23] It was proposed to have a ceasefire with the Maoists and arrange for elections to the Constituent Assembly. The issues that were important for the new government were constituent assembly, political stability and status of monarchy and peaceful resolution of armed conflict.

SPA - Maoist Agreement

The negotiations of the seven party's alliance with the Maoists finally reached to an eight point agreement along with a code of conduct. The agreement included framing an interim constitution, the establishment of an interim government, which will take up the task to conduct elections for the Constituent Assembly, issues relating to disarming the Maoist forces, the future of Maoist army and peace building. The code of conduct included the cessation of armed Maoist forces in rural areas, release of Maoist prisoners by the government, disbandment of parallel government of Maoists and return of underground Maoists.[24]

The interim government took a number of decisions to disarm the king. His powers and political privileges have been taken back. The Hindu status of the state has been withdrawn. Although it was not clear whether the SPA was still looking for a role of monarchy. In this regard Prime Minister G.P. Koirala's opinion further created confusion.

The framing of an interim constitution is in progress. The process of elections for the Constituent Assembly will take some more time. The question of managing the Maoist army, its status and seeking international mediation for this purpose is a more vital question at the moment. The problems identified in the post-conflict transformation Nepal seem to be:

1. The Republican state of Nepal,
2. Having a secular state,
3. Ethnic and regional issues in governance and the question of a federal state,
4. Special rights to dalits and dealing with the gender question,
5. Revolutionary land reforms and economic development with equity,
6. Pursuance of independent economic policy,
7. Scientific and people oriented education system,
8. Management of the Maoist army,
9. Employment and poverty alleviation.

Some of these issues need a long-term planning while others need an immediate concern. A further analysis of some these issues and emerging trends would help us in understanding the direction of Nepali politics.

Emerging Issues and Challenges

The future of Nepali democratic process is yet not certain. Nevertheless, both the Maoists and the political parties have shown dynamism and flexibility. It is after such a long time, experiencing so many ups and downs that the political parties of Nepal agreed in the 12- point understanding, for a non-monarchical constitutional framework. On the other hand, the Maoists agreed to shift from underground to overground.[25] The decision to give up insurgency and participate in the democratic process was highly significant and appreciable. It can be a decision of far reaching consequences. It can prove to be an example and a lesson to insurgents in South Asia or elsewhere.

However, these events have given rise to a situation where many complex problems are coming up that have to be sorted out in order to move ahead smoothly.

I. The Maoists have exhibited a radical shift from insurgency to democratic dispensation. Is it or will it be acceptable to all the Maoist cadres is one issue that has been raised in certain quarters. It is not relevant at the moment. However, in future taking into consideration the fragmentations in the communist movement in Nepal such questions may come up and become relevant in the political discourse of the country.

II. Gyanendra a highly ambitious monarch took the course of Nepali politics after the sad demise of King Birendra. Has he become totally non-influential in the present phase of Nepali politics? How are the traditional forces reacting to the upcoming political situation in Nepal? There is a need to be cautious on this issue. One has to understand that there was a row in Nepal when it was decided to declare the country a secular state. The political parties – Maoist alliance needs to work skillfully, not providing any opportunity for the reactivation of traditional forces. It would be unfounded to assume that the royalist forces will not try to strike back in any form, at least during the interim period. Much would depend on the smooth installation of the new political order and the understanding between SA and Maoists.

III. So to emphasize again the seven party political alliance and the Maoist understanding is the core of upcoming political designs in the country. Maintaining this understanding is a crucial and sensitive issue. The interim period is not that short. It may take not less than two years to finally give a constitution to the country. This is going to be a difficult phase. It is essential that the two groups adhere to the understanding they have reached to. It would be too early to think of what happened in Russia in 1917 and the October revolution. But Maoists may threaten to take up arms again if the understanding is not implemented smoothly. Therefore, there is a need for mature, flexible and farsighted leadership on both sides.

IV. There have occurred instances of lack of coordination between the Maoists and the political parties. The two groups differed over the issue of managing arms of the Maoists. The government holds that the political issues will be discussed after the arms are managed, while the Maoists argue that political issues be discussed first and arms will be managed later on. The two groups had later agreed in August 2006 to write a joint letter to the UN to supervise arms management. However, it reflected lack of coordination between the two.

Koirala has also been alleged of favouring the monarchy. Prime Minister Koirala said that the fringe political parties, Maoists and monarchy should be given a space in democracy so as to prevent them from frustration. This aroused strong reactions among Maoists. Babu Ram Bhattarai said, "We want to caution and warn him (Koirala) that we will be compelled to leave if the government continues to protect the king." There is a need to avoid such tendencies. There is a need for confidence building.

V. The role of international community is also important at this juncture. India and the United States are important players. India has given economic assistance to Nepal. Koirala has visited India and this indicates that the Nepali Congress enjoys India's support. But India has not given any indication of its perception. The United States of America has also announced huge aid to Nepal. They have also offered to train the Nepali army for its civilian relationship. But US has doubted the Maoist commitment to join mainstream politics. The US has not removed Maoists form its list of terrorist. It would depend whether Maoists give up arms or not. The United States has its own vested interest. The international community needs to watch the process cautiously to see that things move smoothly but it is necessary that refrain from any kind of indulgence in the affairs of the country. It seems that UN is the only international agency whose assistance would be secured. However, it might not be possible to ignore the attitude of the major international actors.

The fundamental issue before the interim government along with the Maoists is to constitute the constituent Assembly and prepare a new constitution. There are many expectations and many issues are coming up. A brief overview of some of these issues would help in understanding the likely scenario emerging in Nepal in the process of CA formation and the constitution formation subsequently.

I. How to move towards the constituent Assembly is the foremost issue. There is an understanding that the elections to the Constituent Assembly will be held in near future. How should it operate much depends on the composition of the CA? Will all the forces be abided by the composition of the CA? In the present political scenario it is hardly possible for any party to obtain majority in the CA. In such conditions, it would become all the more necessary that the political forces remain united. The foremost issue before the CA would be to decide for a democratic republic or constitutional monarchy. It seems that the option of a republican constitution will alone ensure peace and stability in Nepal.

II. As pointed above the question of monarchy is important in deciding future political set up. Koirala's inclination to give monarchy a space has already been reacted strongly. Why Koirala uttered these words? It is true that there are sympathizers and supporters of monarchy. But more than that this has been the core of Nepali Political culture. There has always been a conflict between traditional political norms and dynamism of democracy. The democratic forces have lacked self-confidence and faith. This has caused ambiguity in their perception and attitude.

Apart from the Maoists who are strong opponent of the continuation of the institution of monarchy, there are people of civil society who also believe that the monarchy has become irrelevant. They strongly utter that the fruits of people's movement should not be wasted. Devendra Raj Pandey, a prominent civil society leader says, "if the monarchy survives even if in a damaged form, it will strike back again and again, so let us build democratic institutions slowly and have faith in them."

So the fate of monarchy is going to be a debatable issue in the exercise on new constitution. One possibility is that a referendum may take place in this regard.

III. Secularism vis-a-vis Hinduism will be another major issue for the consideration of the new CA. All the constitution of Nepal so far declared Nepal a Hindu state. But it never meant that Nepal was a religious state. It seems that the purpose of declaring Nepal a Hindu state was to carry on the traditional religio-cultural identity of the state and thus serve the political interest of the traditional political elite. It is going to be an important issue in the forthcoming constitution making process. The dalits, ethnic groups and the Maoists will press hard to declare Nepal a secular state in the new constitution. It should be understood properly that the traditional political forces tried to create an ambiguity. There is no need for the political forces to carry with this ambiguity.

IV. The question of federal structure of the Nepali state may also come up in the Constituent Assembly or later on. Suresh Ali Magar one ethnic leader has raised the issue of rights of ethnic minority communities. The different ethnic groups, particularly the people of Mongoloid origin have been demanding their proper representation in the politico-administrative structures. They had also suggested dividing Nepal into 12 autonomous regions. Thus, the agenda of restructuring of the Nepali state seems to be important and likely to come up one way or the other.

V. The question of the status of army will be important for the Constituent Assembly. Traditionally royal Nepal army had allegiance to the palace. Since 2001 army was given the task to contain the insurgency. It was for the first time that army had exposure of such a kind. In the new constitution question will arise to whom army pledge allegiance. The civil-military relationship will also be an important issue.

A related issue here is about Maoist army. What should be done to it? Many suggestions have come up: that it should be merged with the royal army. Another idea is that it should be given a distinct status as a pera-military force. It is also being said that it should be dismantled and the Maoist rebels be given employment.

VI. The stability and democracy not only depends on a smooth political process but it essentially requires a socio-economic process ensuring development with equity. Therefore, the socio-economic agenda is also going to be important in the new constitution. Nepal's problems and challenges of development are complex. It has been a resource poor land locked state. How Maoists are going to address themselves to the issues of globalisation, privatization and external involvement in Nepal's development is a significant issue. Similarly the question of land reforms, regional disparities and gender are vital.

VII. The question of provision of right to revolt has also come up. It is being said that the constitution has to ensure that no Nepali is discriminated and suppressed in the name of religion, ethnicity and so on.

VIII. How the new Constituent Assembly is going to address itself to the question of dalits is also important. The dalit movement is gradually coming up in Nepal. The question of reservation to dalits may come up.

IX. The question of Nepal's foreign policy dynamics will also significantly come up for the consideration of the Constituent Assembly. Here the issue of Nepal's relations with the neighbouring countries is most significant. The Nepali Congress is known for its leaning towards India. The Maoists have been demanding revoking unequal treaties. Their reference is to 1950 Indo-Nepal treaty of Peace and Friendship. Similarly the issue of open border with India is also important. Is there any alternative framework of foreign policy is an important question.

There are many issues and many problems. Many of them are realities of a multi-structured society of Nepal. There is no need to shy away from these issues. It would be in the long-term interest of the country that these issues and problems are properly addressed. It can be said that the institutionalization and growth of democracy will depend to which extent these issues are resolved.

REFERENCES

1. J.K. Sinha, "Misreading the Mood, India Fails to understand Maoist insurgency in Nepal", *The Times of India,* November 12, 2005.
2. Sidharth Vardarajan, "In Nepal, the Beginning of an End", *Hindu,* April 22, 2006.
3. For the text of his speech see, *Kathmandu Post,* February 2, 2005.
4. Manjushree Thapa, "Nepal's Troubled Kingdom", *Hindu,* April 23, 2006
5. Michael Hutt, "Nepal and Bhutan in 2005, Monarchy and Democracy can they Coexist", *Asian Survey,* Vol. XLVI, No. 1, January–February 2006: 120.
6. Michael Hutt, N. 5: 121.
7. See for details, *Kathmandu Post,* May 9, 2005.
8. See, *Nepal Weakly,* Vol. 6, No. 15, November 20, 2005.
9. *The Hindustan Times,* November 7, 2005.
10. Bishnu Raj Upreti, *Armed Conflict and Peace Process in Nepal,* Adroit Publishers, New Delhi, 2006: 349.
11. *The Hindustan Times,* February 9, 2006.
12. *The Hindustan Times,* April 24, 2006.
13. Manjushree Thapa, N. 4.
14. *The Hindustan Times,* April 19, 2006.
15. N. 14.
16. *The Hindustan Times,* April 21, 2006.
17. Nilooa Roy Chaudhary, "The Great Indian Balancing Act", *The Hindustan Times,* April 23, 2006.
18. *The Hindustan Times,* April 24, 2006.
19. *Hindu,* April 22, 2006.
20. *Hindu,* April 26, 2006.
21. *The Hindustan Times,*_April 26, 2006.
22. *The Hindustan Times,* April 29, 2006.
23. N. 22.
24. Sita Ram Yechury, "Learning from Experience an Analysis of Contesting

Approaches of Maoists in Nepal and India", *Economic and Political Weekly,* July 22 2006: 3170–71.

25. For an analysis of Maoist movement and the emerging issues see, Saroj Giri, "Social Transformation and Political Power, Maoists in Nepal", *Economic and Political Weekly,* May 27, 2006.

Websites

www. Nepaldemocracy.org

url:http//nepalresearch.com

www.insec-nepal.com

www.ibcs.org/hmt/milgro

www.ups/maoist-nep.html

www.asianet.com

9

Post Script
On the Path to Democracy: Challenges and Prospects

Nepal is passing through a transitional phase. Fast developments are taking place in the country since the April 2006 political change. The democratic forces are aspiring for a stable-liberal political system. The Maoists who have given up the revolutionary path and responding to the constitutional-democratic means in a positive direction are looking forward for the realization of their goals. The trends are being set towards that direction on the basis of a closer understanding between the democratic forces and the Maoists. However, this transitional phase is very crucial for Nepal. It is true that fast developments are taking place towards democratic stabilization. But long distance has still to be travelled to attain the goals of state restructuring and democratic order. There are a number of challengers; and there are lingering fears and doubts. Despite of the polarization of rightist and leftist forces there are conflicting interests and contesting identities. There are forces in the country that may play a destabilizing role. Therefore, the ongoing processes of stability have problems and challenges. It would be desirable here to understand the new developments in Nepali politics and the upcoming trends and the challenges ahead.

Maoists Extending the Ceasefire

After the formation of the seven party alliance interim government under the leadership of Nepali Congress leader G.P. Koirala, the main issue was to bring the Maoists in the Interim Government. It required resolution of certain issues relating to surrendering of arms by the Maoists, finalization of the interim constitution etc. It is true that the Seven Party Alliance (SPA) had succeeded in persuading the Maoists to follow a constitutional path and join hands with the democratic forces in order to realize goals of a new Nepal. There were many complicated issues and that had delayed the understanding to which both the groups were expected to reach. The Maoists once again established their commitment to the peace process by declaring a three months extension to ceasefire on 29 October, 2006.[1] The ceasefire was much in need because talks were still going on between the SPA and the Maoist leaders and any agreement was yet to come out on the current political situation in the country. It is true that both the groups were not clear in respect to the understanding that was to be developed in order to promote peace, stability and democracy in the country; the ceasefire provided an opportunity to continue the on going process. Moreover, there were forces that were still looking at the peace process with doubts. So the Maoist ceasefire was an important development.

Ideological Synthesis

The Maoists of Nepal emerged as a revolutionary party and launched a 'people's war' with the objectives of restructuring the state and transformation of the society. They succeeded in bringing up these issues on the national agenda. But what can be considered as a tremendous achievement is the fact that the Maoists have chosen a democratic path for this purpose along with the democratic forces of Nepal.[2] During the course of insurgency Maoists gave an understanding of a revolutionary group that was looking for a complete change in Nepal through revolutionary means. They did talk of a republic state in Nepal but issues were not very clear in ideological terms. The ideological contents whether in the form of 'Prachanda Path' or other issues were directed towards a revolutionary struggle to attain the goals stet by them to bring a political change in the country. The Maoist leaders are gradually trying to synthesise their ideology in favour of a democratic political order. They have been talking of incorporating the ideas of Mahatma Gandhi, Lord Buddha and Karl Marx in their policies and actions. It broadly means that they now believe in a humanitarian, socialistic and democratic approach that would primarily focus upon the welfare of the people. Maoist leader Pushp Kamal Dahal (Prachanda) in an interview in New Delhi said that "Gautam Buddha has given a call from here for the ideological synthesis of humanity, we now want to give a new ideological message for the new world."[3]

Maoists have been talking of a new democracy (Navlo Janbad) in Nepal. But it is not much elaborated. It appears that they would aspire for a communitarian democracy in which all the identities regions, groups and communities are associated in the national political process on an equalitarian basis. Their emphasis is that democracy should not remain a mere formality. It must work for bringing economic equality and social justice and change the lives of the people. Babu Ram Bhattarai in an interview recently said, "The Communists had tried out people's democracy in Russia and China we want to try out a new model which will incorporate the ideas of Gandhi, Marx, Lenin and be a synthesis of all."[4]

Prachanda during his recent visit to India also give the impression that they should not be equated with the Naxalities and the other revolutionary groups in India. It seems that on the basis of this distinction they would justify their ideology of democracy and democratic governance as a means to social transformation. In fact, the Maoists joining the constitutional-democratic path indicates that their revolutionary path was more a strategy to open up possibilities for a political change rather than a social movement/revolution aimed at completely uprooting of the socio-political order. The Maoist leaders have also tried to differentiate themselves from the other movements in South Asia. They believe that the major problem with the movement of LITTE in Sri Lanka in that it has been based on a narrow nationalist approach. It has lacked ideological and political contexts in its struggle against the Sri Lanka state. The fact remains that the LITTE has followed a separatist movement while Maoists were a political movement aimed at restructuring the state.

The way Maoist leaders have tried to look at the movement of LITTE shows that the Maoists would believe in a broad based nationalism, which would be secular and democratic in its approach and contents.

Besizing the King

There has been lot of resentment in Nepal against the monarchy after the February 2005 coup. It is for the first time that the people of Nepal have expressed their dissatisfaction against the monarchy and accused king Gyanendra for misusing the powers and relegating the powers and prestige of monarchy to the lowest web. It is for the first time that the people have lost their faith on monarchy in such a massive way. After the April 2006 change one of the main dimension of the Nepali politics has been to withdraw powers of the king and make the monarchy ineffective in the politics of the country. It has not been viewed sufficient to disarm king Gyanendra politically. There has been a strong opinion that King Gyanendra and his associates had done lot of atrocities on people during his direct rule.

Nepali Government constituted a commission under the Chairmanship of justice Krishna Jung Rayamajhi to recommend action against 202 people including king Gyanendra. Justice Krishna Jung Rayamajhi submitted its report to the government on 20 November 2006. The commission held King Gyanendra responsible for the atrocities on the people at the time of April 2006 pro-democracy movement. It was also recommended that action be taken against King Gyanendra not in his capacity as the King but as the then head of the State. The Chairman of the Committee said, "We have decided to recommend the Parliament to take necessary steps against the King as we found him guilty."[5] It was also clarified that though King Gyanendra did not respond to the question – are send by the commission it does not mean to say that he did no wrong.[6] It is for the first time that a commission was constituted against a King that has found him guilty.

The Government decided to form a five-member committee to recommend action against the King. The Committee has not yet submitted its report. The fate of the monarchy will ultimately be decided in the referendum. But if the current developments are any indication, the institution of monarchy has lost its credibility and the way to its come back is extremely difficult. As far King Gyanendra is concerned there are still people in Nepal who would look for a minimum status to the monarchy in the new political set up, but it is difficult to state whether they would be able to reverse the trends. It can be said t! t the role played by King Gyanendra has proved to be detrimental to the institution of monarchy in Nepal. It seems that King Gyanendra in his capacity, as the then head of the State is likely pay for all that happened during his direct rule.

Six-Point Agreement

Three issues were important in order to take the political process ahead towards democracy and stability in Nepal. These were: settlement of the question of Maoist army, and weapons and also at the same time to tied down the royal Nepali army possessed by them; finalization of the interim constitution; and the joining of

Maoists in the Interim Government. These steps were necessary in order to set a stage for the elections to the Constituent Assembly.

After several rounds of talks between the SPA and Maoist leaders a six-point agreement was signed between the two parties. [7] There were suspicions, delays and misunderstanding but it was ultimately signed on 21 November, 2006 It has following aspects:

1. The Maoist armed cadres will be kept in seven cantonments and their arms will be kept in the designated cantonments. The Maoist leaders will keep the keys to the lockers where arms are kept. A team of the United Nations will monitor the locks using a closed vault camera and an electronic sensor device. A new military act will be prepared to ensure that control of the army rests with the elected representatives in the Government.
2. Agreed to decide future of Monarchy by the first meeting of the Constituent Assembly through a simple majority of vote. The property acquired by King Gyanendra by virtue of ascending the throne will be nationalized. The private property will remain with him. The property of assassinated King Birendra and his family will be kept under a trust and will be utilized for the purpose of national welfare.
3. An Interim Government lead by PM G.P. Koirala of Nepali Congress Party will be formed by December.
   The agreement did not mention any thing about the composition of the cabinet, its size, etc. It seems that it was left for mutual discussions and agreement.
4. The two parties agreed on the formation of an interim legislature consisting of 330 members. The party-wise breakup would be: Nepali Congress: 75, Maoist = 73, Nepali Congress (Democratic) = 42. 48 members will be nominated from among senior political figures, civil society and professional bodies. The smaller political parties will also be given representation in the interim legislature.
5. It has been agreed that the Constituent Assembly will have 425 members. 205 members will be elected from the existing parliamentary constituencies on the first–part–the post system. 204 will be nominated by the political parties in proportion to the popular votes they receive in the elections to the Constituent Assembly.

6. It has been agreed to work for the socio-economic transformation in the country and restructuring of state. There is a commitment to eradicate inequalities.

It is believed that the agreement has paved a way for the Maoist to join the Interim Government. It can be added here that this agreement is important because the two groups have succeeded in deciding over the issues that are important to take the peace process further and decide the future course of politics in the country.

Interim Constitution

The Seven Parties Alliance and Maoists have also agreed on the interim constitution. The Interim Constitution had been though prepared earlier, the two groups were yet to accord their consent to the Constitution.

The Interim Constitution has 169 articles. It has been decided that the Interim Constitution will be formally promulgated once the management of the Maoist army cadres and weapons is complete. It will remain effective till a new constitution is framed by the Constituent Assembly, which is likely to come in to existence next summer.

The Interim Constitution has declared Nepal a multi-cultural state.

The most important feature of the Interim Constitution is that the Prime Minister will be the head of the Government as well as the head of the State. The King is stripped of all positions in the Government. He will not remain even the ceremonial head of the State. This the 6th statute of Nepal first being in 1948 declared by the Rana Prime Minister Padma Shaumsher JBR to firm up total rule by his clan and the last (5th) in 1990 to list ban on political parties. The PM is authorized to use all powers hitherto exercised by the King.

The Interim Constitution providers a number of rights to the Nepali people such as right to education, employment, health as basic rights and then right against untouchability, right to social security, prosperity, religion, culture, right against torture, right to information and right to adequate wages.

It also provides for the directive principles of state policies.

There will be constitutional council that will recommend appointments to various constitutional bodies.

A six member Security Council has been constituted to mobilize the royal army. Earlier royal army also uses to be a member of the Security Council but now there is not place for it in the Council.

The Interim Constitution has also made provision for an interim legislature as per agreement between SPA and Maoists.

Regarding the Constituent Assembly it states that its will be elected on the basis of one man-one vote on the basis on the adult franchise (18 years).The Constituent Assembly is suppose to complete its task of framing a constitution of Nepal in two years time.

The Interim Constitution is an important document and with its promulgation one phase of the current political process will be completed. But as has been pointed earlier, there are many crucial issues and turning points that have to be settled and dealt with carefully before Nepal reaches to the final stage of democracy peace and stability. Hence, there are issues that need to be taken care of by both the SPA and Maoists. A few of then may be discussed here.

Problems and Prospects

Despite many ups and downs a political process has been set up which would take Nepal towards democracy, peace and stability as its ultimate goals. It is necessary that this process is not detailed or subverted. The primary responsibility goes to the SPA and the Maoists. But it is also the responsibility of other political parties and groups, organizations of the country to share this responsibility. The intellectuals, academic institutions and media need to lend their support in a positive direction. The civil society in Nepal needs to take it into consideration that the process of peace building is not left to the SPA and the Maoists alone. The civil society has a role to play in this process. It is the responsibility of the civil society to keep a watch on the democratic forces and keep them on the right track.

There has been lot of talks on the restructuring of state and transformation of the Nepali society, particularly in the post-April 2006 period.[8] Nepal needs restructuring of the state and transformation of the society, there cannot be any second opinion about that. The agenda of the restructuring of the state is clear. Maoists have been talking about abolition of the monarchic state and declaring Nepal a republic state. This itself is a major step towards restructuring the state. The new constitution that would follow in the light of a republic state would resolve the other issues relating to the restructuring of the state. But one thing must be clear to all democratic forces and Maoists that the removal of the monarchy from the political scenario and declaration of a republican state alone would not serve the purpose. Republic state in itself is not an end. It can only be an instrument to attain the objective of restructuring the state. It has also to be borne in mind that the democratic forces have to look at the changes in the Nepali political dynamics in a broader perspective. Just stick to the objective to relegate the king to a common man would be a narrow approach. The broader approach should be to restructuring the state and declaring Nepal a republican state is only a primary step in that direction.

As far the transformation of the society is concerned it is a long process. There has to be a clear agenda for social transformation. So far no clear agenda has come forward in this regard. So there is a need to concentrate on these aspects as well and draw a clear perspective. Clear trends have to be set with strong structural arrangements to start process of social transformation.

The political parties that have exhibited fragmentation and group fightings need to show solidarity and farsightedness. They will have to rise above the politics of opportunism, which has been the style and attitude of most of the parties in near past. Most of the political parties lack ideological strength and sound social bases. Parties will have to look in to these issues with all seriousness. Their own strength and capability is the strength of democracy. There is a need for farsighted political leadership. There is also need for a national consensus among different democratic forces on the issues relating to democratic governance in the country. The political parties have a major role to play in inculcating a democratic political culture. So it is necessary that the political parties move on a right direction with a right approach.

The Maoists who have been a revolutionary party few month back have opted for a democratic course. It is indeed a tremendous achievement. But it is necessary for the Maoists to transform themselves as a democratic force in real terms. Maoists are a major political force today. But they need to avoid pressure politics and develop tolerance and mutual understanding.

The role of bureaucracy is important in the present process of peace building in Nepal. The Nepali bureaucracy has been narrowly represented in the past. It has been labelled as Gork-hali bureaucracy to an organization that has represented upper class hill people. These facts can no more be ignored and the task of broadening and liberalization of bureaucracy has to be given a serious thought.

These issues are important in the context of peace building in Nepal. Much of the task of democratic order and stability would rest on how these issues are dealt with.

It is certain that whether it is the formation of the Constituent Assembly, or the new constitution and so on the future directions of Nepali Politics would rest on an understanding and mutual co-operation between the political parties and the Maoists.

REFERENCES

1. *Stateman,* November 3, 2006.
2. *Economic and Political Weekly,* November 18, 2006 Editorial: 4711.
3. *Hindustan Times,* November 20, 2006.
4. N. 3.
5. *Asian Age,* November 16, 2006.
6. N. 5.
7. See, *Hindu,* November 9, 2006.
8. B.C.Upreti, "State and Society in Nepal: Issues in and Challenges of Restructuring the State and Transforming the Society", paper presented at an International Seminar on Democracy and Development in Nepal.

   BHU, Varanasi, 18-19 December, 2006.
   http//www.India New.
   http//www. Daily India.com
   http//www.voanews.com

10
Conclusion

Democracy that evolved in the west has become a popular form of governance all over the world. It has a long and curious history. There does not appear to be any alternative to democracy that would ensure popular participation, freedom and rights. However, in its journey over centuries, democracy itself has produced many alternative forms. As a result the history of democracy is puzzling. Every country today in the world claims that it is democratic no matter to what extent it fulfills the basic contours of democracy; no matter its views are centrist, rightist or leftist. For many democracy is only a means of seeking popular legitimacy in the arena of politics. This is how an autocrat or a military dictator seeks popular legitimacy and without any hesitation calls itself a democracy.

Right since the times of Aristotle there have been political thinkers who were very critical of the theory and practice of democracy. The earlier thinkers on democracy tried to put forward an ideal form of democracy like ... of the people, by the people for the people. But in practice there were many complications. In most of the countries democracy remained a majoritarian rule. This has been problematic in the plural societies. So how can democracy acquire the shape of a communitarian rule is a major problem today. Democracy has to be representative and participatory in which all the groups, communities and regions are involved.

A state may have democracy but the history of their political institutions reveals the fragility and vulnerability of democratic arrangements and practices. It is because of the fact that either the socio-economic bases of democracy are weak or that the majoritarian community ignores the interest of the minorities. It is in such a complex situation that it becomes difficult to sustain democracy. Actually, in democracy the constraints of social stratification always produce protests against inequalities. Sometimes these protests are based on the inherent discriminations and inequalities created by the state. But at times these protests are artificially created as a part of the power game. In both the cases, it becomes an imperative need for the state to respond to these protests and resolve them amicably. If the state succeeds in resolving these issues democracy will be sustained if not more challenges to democracy will creep up. Therefore, democracy requires a civil society that is strong enough to resolve conflicts of diverse interests at its own level; a civil society that has the capacity to act as a balancing force between state and society; a civil society which is solid enough to resist uncalled and unwanted state in various over society. The growth of such a civil society is possible when the society is developed on the basis of equity and fraternity and the economy that has the capacity to deliver goods to the people and provide equal opportunities to all over its resources. Thus, democracy has to be a multi-dimensional project. It is not sufficient to create constitutional and political structures. It is very essential that the country has a developed society and developed economy. Only through equitable social and economic development compounded with political freedom and rights that a civil society grows. A strong civil society is the greatest asset to democracy.

II

In the South Asian region democracy is a phenomenon of the post-colonialism. It was during the struggle against the British colonial rule that the political leaders of the South Asia came in touch of the democratic experiences of the western societies. The constitutional reforms that were introduced in India by the British rulers also proved to be India's apprenticeship with democracy. It was obvious that the South Asian states adopted British model of democracy. It is interesting that except in India, other countries of South Asia failed in the sustenance of democracy. India had a long history of National Movement that also produced political parties, political leadership, constitutions and political representation in a crude form. India also had administrative and judicial structures, social reforms and infrastructural development. It is because of this background that India could adhere to a secular democratic system, which others did not due to inadequate social and economic bases for the successful working of democracy.

The idea of democracy came to Nepal in 1950 through an Anti-Rana movement followed by a tripartite agreement that actually laid the foundation of democracy. But this foundation proved to be hollow partly because of the nature of the agreement that allowed the traditional political forces to perpetuate and partly due to the prevailing socio-economic conditions in the country. It is true that some short of political awakening had begun in Nepal against the autocratic rule of Ranas, largely organized from the Indian soil. But Nepal lacked any long drawn movement for the installation of democracy in the country. Neither the pro-democratic forces of the country had any apprenticeship in democracy as the Indian democratic forces had. The political parties which were founded in the Indian soil could not gain any chance to organize themselves in the Nepali soil and lay down a strong foundation for themselves. Before that would happen a movement against the Rana rule began and before the movement would take any concrete shape it was abandoned dramatically followed by the New Delhi agreement.

There were four important factors affecting working of democracy in Nepal in the post-1950 period.

I. There was not a total transfer of powers from the traditional rulers to the democratic forces. The traditional political elite was not only allowed a share in the power structure but the responsibility for the installation of democracy was given to it. In subsequent years the traditional political forces utilized the situation in consolidating its own powers instead of strengthening democratic forces. Thus the history of democracy in Nepal was marked by a conflict between traditional and modern-democratic forces in which the traditional forces were in an advantageous position. So the democracy had to suffer.

II. Except for an interim constitution, no concrete efforts were made to institutionalize democracy in the country in the years immediately following the 1950 political change.

III. The Political parties lacked any short of experience in democratic governance. They also did not have a strong organizational base in the country. So in comparison to the traditional political elite their position was quite weak. On the contrary the traditional forces had strong support base and once they began to consolidate their powers the feudal elements extended their support to these forces in stead of the modern democratic forces.

IV. The Nepalese society was feudal to the core, which would hardly have supported the process of democratization in the country. Its vested interest was in the perpetuation of the traditional political elite.

V. There was no social and economic support base for the operationalisation of democracy.

All these factors went in favour of the traditional political elite and democracy had to suffer at its hands for a long time.

However, it was not possible for the Nepalese rulers to ignore the resurgence of Asian and African countries. It was apparent that it was difficult to sustain the authoritarian rule without some short of a democratic cover. Secondly, it was also difficult to ignore the revolution of rising expectations in the post-colonial phase that had taken into grip most of the newly independent countries. Hence, it became an imperative need to introduce certain socio-economic reforms. The monarchy though himself became an agent of modernization and the benefits of the development largely went to the feudal class, it was not possible to contain the consciousness that these efforts at modernization and development (even if they were controlled) brought in the Nepali society.

It is due to the contradictory policies of the monarchy to control the political change but to allow socio-economic change that the democratic forces remain alive in the country. They succeeded in reinforcing democracy in the country as the situation gave way to the polarization of democratic forces. However, the working of democracy and the process of its institutionalization has been rather disappointing. The democratic elite have not yet succeeded in taking the reigns of power independently. It has to share power with the traditional political elite in one way or the other. In the process the democratic elite has turned to be subservient to the traditional elite because the socio-economic context the historical antecedents and the political culture has favoured them. The democratic elite cannot strengthen itself unless it becomes the independent stakeholder of power and politics in Nepal. The feudalistic orientation of the Nepali society and economy will remain alive so long as the traditional political elite will have stakes in power politics. So the institutionalization of democracy in a long-term perspective will require emergence of democratic forces as independent stakeholder of politics and the comprehensive socio-economic transformation. These are indeed inter-related phenomenon and would sustain each other in the process.

III

What course democracy is likely to take up in Nepal and what is the future of democracy in that country is the question that should agitate most of the minds in Nepal and elsewhere in the academics. Let me first make it clear to those who believe that democracy is not possible in Nepal are in under illusion. The recent movement for democracy has made it clear that there are strong impulses for democracy in the country. Whatever breakdown occurred democracy has revived in Nepal again. But one has to take in to consideration that the long-term sustenance of democracy is like to remain a complex project in Nepal. Even if the Nepali progressive forces succeed in envisaging a republican democracy for the country there has to take place a comprehensive social and economic transformation in the country. This becomes a primary requirement given the present state of Nepali society. But it is not possible to restructure a feudalistic society overnight. It will take time. So in the near future there does not appear to be any escape from a fragile democracy in the country.

The political parties and the political leadership are the main vehicles of democratic governance. What Nepal or for that matter any democratic state requires is an ideologically and organizationally strong political parties. Though political parties alone cannot be held responsible for the problems of democracy and good governance in Nepal, it has to be realized that it was the weaknesses of the political parties that provided space to other forces in the arena of politics. The political parties were marginalized and so was the democratic order. Can political parties learn from the past is a big question. Unless there is a self-realization idioms of Nepali politics will not change much. The political parties need to create a balance between the quest for power and ideological commitments.

There is a need for a strong and forward looking political leadership. The political leadership has been largely responsible for internal political conflicts of parties and destabilizing tendencies in politics. The leadership has to rise above to partitioned politics. The concept of collective leadership has not succeeded in Nepal.

What is important is how to insulate a democratic political culture in Nepal? Of course, the democratic culture is not something which can be imposed on the society from above. It is a question of popular perception, values and norms. So it has to grow in the society. It can be possible only when the democratic state is capable enough to deliver goods to the people as per their requirements. The state, parties and the civil society has an important role to play in this regard. Democracy can survive only in a society which has a democratic culture.

Nepal has still to travel a long way on the path to build democracy. One would only hope that this process is on now and the country will not require yet another struggle for democracy.

Select Bibliography

Arblaster, Anthony, *Democracy*, World View Press, Delhi, 1997.

Almond, Gabriel and Verba, Sydney, *The Civic Culture, Political Attitudes and Democracy in Five Nations*, Princeton University Press, Princeton, 1963.

________(ed.), *The Civic Culture, Revisited*, Boston, 1980.

Baral, Lok Raj (ed.), *Nepal Political Parties and Parliament*, Adroit Publishers, Delhi, 2006.

________, *The Facets of Maoist Insurgency in Nepal*, Adroit Publishers, Delhi, 2006.

________ (ed.), *Leadership in Nepal*, Adroit Publishers, Delhi, 2001.

Barlal, L.S., "Changing Constitutional and Political System of Nepal", *Foreign Affairs Report* (New Delhi), January, 1977.

Baucher, Jean, *Democracy, an Analytical Survey*, NBT, New Delhi, 1998.

Bhattarai, Babu Ram, *The Nature of Underdevelopment and Regional Structure of Nepal*, Adroit Publishers, Delhi, 2003.

Bista Dor Bahadur, *Fatalism and Development, Nepal's Struggle for Modernisation*, Orient Longman, Calcutta, 1991.

Borre Ole *et al.*, *Nepali Political Behaviour*, Sterling Publishers, Delhi, 1999.

Brown Louise, T., *The Challenge of Democracy in Nepal – A Political History*, Routledge, London, 1996.

Chand, Diwakar, *Essays on Development of Nepal*, Chandni Publications, Kathmandu, 2003.

Chaudhary, Nilobia Roy, "The Great Indian Balancing Act", *The Hindustan Times*, April 23, 2006.

Dahal, Dev Raj, *Conflict Situation in Nepal*, FES, Kathmandu, 2004.

Dahal, Madan, K. (ed.), *Future of Nepalese Economy*, NEFAS, Kathmandu, 1993.

Datt, P., *Indian Democracy, New Challenges*, Kanishka Publications, New Delhi, 1996.

Diamond, Larry (ed.), *Democracy in Asia*, Boulder Colorado, 1989.

Fisher Margarat, W. and Rose Lao E., *Politics of Nepal, Persistence and Change in an Asian Monarchy*, Cornell University Press, Ithaca, 1971.

Gaize Fredrick, H., *Regionalism and National Unity in Nepal*, California University Press, Berkeley, 1975.

Gellener David, N. (ed.), *Nationalism and Ethnicity in a Hindu Kingdom: The Politics of Culture in Contemporary Nepal*, Harwood Academic Publications, Amsterdam, 1997.

Giri Saroj, "Social Transformation and Political Power, Maoists in Nepal", *Economic and Political Weekly*, May 27, 2006.

Gupta, Anirudh, *Politics in Nepal*, Bombay, 1964.

Gurung, D.B. (ed.), *Nepal Tomorrow, Voices and Vision*, Kathmandu, 2003.

Gurung, Harka, *Nepal, Social Demography and Expressions*, NEW ERA, Kathmandu, 1998.

Hachhethu, Krishna, *State of Democracy in Nepal*, SDSA/N, Kathuru, 2004.

Hachhethu, Krishna, *Party Building in Nepal, Organisation Leadership and People*, Mandala Book Point, Kathmandu, 2002.

Hayer Louis D., "The Monarchy and Modernization in Nepal", *Asian Survey*, Vol. XV, No. 7, 39, 1975.

Hoften Martin *et. al.*, *People, Politics and Ideology, Democracy and Social Change in Nepal*, Mandala Book Point, Kathmandu, 1999.

Hold David, *Models of Democracy*, Polity Press, Oxford, 1993.

Huntington Samuel P. and Nelson M., *No Easy Choice, Political Participation in Developing Countries*, Harward University Press, 1967.

Huti Michael, "Nepal and Bhutan in 2005, Monarchy and Democracy can they coexist?" *Asian Survey*, Vol. XLVI, No. 1, January–February, 2006.

________, (ed.), *Nepal in the Nineties*, Oxford University Press, Delhi, 1993.

Inglehart Ronald, "Trust Well Being of Democracy" in Warren mark E. (ed.), *Democracy and Trust*, Cambridge University Press, 1999.

Jha, H.B., *Resource Mobilisation and Economic Development in Nepal During the Plan Period*, Allahabad, 1984.

Joyal, N.C. *Democracy and the State*, Oxford University Press, Berkely, 1966.

Karki, Arjun and Seddon David (eds.), *The People's War in Nepal: The Left Perspective*, Adroit Publishers, Delhi, 2003.

Kumar, Dhrub (ed.), *Domestic Conflict and Crisis of Governability in Nepal*, CNAS, Kathmandu, 2000.

________ (ed.), *State, Leadership and Politics in Nepal*, CNAS, Kathmandu, 1995.

Kohli, Atul (ed.), *India's Democracy*, Princeton University Press, 1988.

________, *Democracy and Discontent, India's Growing Crisis of Governability*, Cambridge University Press, 1990.

Kumar, D.P., *Nepal: A Year of Decision*, Vikas Publishing House, New Delhi, 1980.

Kiyoko Ogura, *Kathmandu Spring: The People's Movement of 1990*, Himal Books, Katamandu, 2001.

Lawati, Mahendra, *Towards a Democratic Nepal: Inclusive Political Institutions for a Multi-Cultural Society*, Sage Publications, New Delhi, 2005.

Lipson Leslie, *The Democratic Civilization*, Oxford University Press, New York, 1964.

Mahat Ram Sharma, *In Defence of Democracy, Dynamics and Fault Lines of Nepal's Political Economy*, Adroit Publishers, Delhi, 2005.

Mahajan Gurpreet, *The Multicultural Path, Issues of Diversity and Discrimination in Democracy*, Sage Publications, New Delhi, 2002.

Mill John Stuart, *On Liberty and Representative Government*, J. M. Dent, London, 1976.

Muni, S.D., *Maoist Insurgency in Nepal*, Delhi, 2005.

Pandey, D.R., *Nepal's Failed Development: Reflections on the Mission and the Melodies*, Nepal South Asia Center, Kathmandu, 1999.

Pandey, Nischal Nath, *Nepal's Maoist Movement and Implications for India and China*, Manohar, Delhi, 2005.

Pandey, Ram Niwas, *Making of Modern Nepal*, Nirala Publishers, New Delhi, 1997.

Regmi Mahesh, C., *A Study in Nepalese Economic History*, New Delhi, 1971.

________, *Land Ownership in Nepal*, California University, Berkeley, 1975.

Regmi, Rishikeshav Raj, *Dimensions of Nepali Culture and Society*, SANN Research Institute, Kathmandu, 1990.

Rosty, Rochard, "Post Modernist Bourgeous Liberalism" in Docherty Thomas (ed.), *Post Modernism: A Reader*, California University Press, New York, 1987.

Samanta, Pranab Dhab, "Nepal Faces King Size Questions", *Indian Express*, April 27, 2006.

Sarton, G., *The Theory of Democracy Revisited*, Chattanm House Publishers, 1987.

Schumpeter, J., *Capitalism, Socialism and Democracy*, Allen and Unwin London, 1976.

Shah, Rishikesh, *Nepali Politics, Retrospect and Prospect*, Oxford University Press, New Delhi, 1978.

________, *Politics in Nepal 1980–90*, Manohar, Delhi, 1990.

________, *Three Decades Two kings 1960–90*, Sterling Publication, Delhi, 1990.

Sheth, D.L. and Nandy, Ashish (eds.), *The Multiverse of Democracy*, Sage Publications, New Delhi, 1996.

Shrestha, Anand Prasad and Upreti, Hari (eds.), *Critical Barriers to the Negotiation of Armed Conflict in Nepal*, Nepal Foundation for Advance Studies, Kathmandu, 2005.

Shrestha, N.R., *In the Name of Development: A Reflection in Nepal*, Educational Enterprises, Kathmandu, 1997.

Sharma, P.R., *The State and Society in Nepal: Historical Foundations and Contemporary Trends*, Himal Books, Kathmandu, 2004.

Sinha, J.K., "Misreading the Mood, India Fails to understand Maoist Crisis in Nepal", *Times of India*, November 12, 2005.

Thapa, Deepak (ed.), *Understanding the Maoist Movement in Nepal*, Martin Chautari, Kathmandu, 2003.

Thapa, Deepak and Sijapati, Bandana, *A Kingdom under Siege: Nepal's Maoist Insurgency*, Martin Chautari, Kathmandu, 2003.

Thapa, Manjushree, "Nepal's Troubled Kingdom", *Hindu*, April 23, 2006.

Thapa, Manjushree, *Forget Kathmandu*, Penguin, Delhi, 2005.

UNDP, *Nepal Human Development: Empowerment and Poverty Reduction*, UNDP Nepal, Kathmandu, 2004.

Upreti, B.C., "Politics of Referendum in Nepal" in: Dharamdasani M.D. (ed.), *Political Participation and Change in South Asia*, Varanasi, 1984.

Upreti, B.C., "Nepal's Panchayat Democracy in Crisis", *Eastern Economist,* January 25, 1980.

_________., "Nepal's Relations with India During the Comunist Regime", *Journal of International Relations* (Dhaka), Vol. 5 Nos, 1&2, July–June 1997-98.

_________., "Monarchy and Nation Building in Nepal" in Chaube S.K. (ed.), *The Himalayas, Profile of Modernisation and Adaptation,* Sterling Publications, New Delhi, 1985.

_________., *Nepal, Dilemma of Development and Change in Far Western Hills,* Indus, New Delhi, 2006.

_________., *Contemporary South Asia,* Kalinga, Delhi 2004.

_________., *Nepali Congress: A Study of its Performance in General Election and Aftermath,* Nirala, Delhi, 1993.

_________., *Uneasy Friends, Readings in India–Nepal Relations,* Kalinga, Delhi, 2001.

_________., "Democracy in Nepal: Bumpy Ground and Road Blocks", in Kulwant Kaur *et al.,* (eds.), *South Asia, Dynamics of Polity, Society and Economy,* Knowledge World, New Delhi, 2006.

_________., "Maoist Insurgency in Nepal Causes and Impact", *South Asian Survey,* January–June, 2006.

_________., "Democracy in South Asia: Nature, Pattern and Constraints", in Dharmadasani M.D. (ed.), *Multi-party Democracy in South Asia,* Anmol Publications, Delhi, 2001.

_________., "Nepal: In Search of Good Governance", *Asian Studies* (Calcutta), Vol. XIX, No. 2, July–December, 2001: 1–38.

_________., "Ethnicity and Politics in Nepal: Emerging Patterns of Socio-Political Mobilisation and Alignments", *South Asian Studies,* Vol. 37, No.1, January–July 2002: 1–35.

_________., "Will Monarchy Survive", *Seminar* 546, April, 2005.

_________., "Democracy in Nepal: Political System in Transition", *Nepali Political Science and Politics* (Kathmandu), Vol. 2, 1993.

_________., "Intra-Party Conflicts Within Nepali Congress: A Study of the 1994, Kathmandu By Election" *South Asian Studies,* January–December, 1996.

_________., "Politics in Nepal; Governmental Stability, Party Cleavages and Crisis of Democracy in the Post-1990 Period", *Asian Panorama,* Vol. 3, Nos. 1 & 2, December, 2004.

Upreti, B.R., "Nepal on Fire: A Tragedy of Betrayal", *South Asian Journal*, Vol. 7, December, 2004.

__________., *The Price of Neglect: From Resource Conflict to Maoist Insurgency in the Himalayan Kingdom*, Bhrikuti Academic Publications, Kathmandu, 2004.

__________., *Armed Conflict and Peace Process in Nepal*, Adroit Publishers, New Delhi, 2006.

Vardarajan, Sidharth, "In Nepal, the Beginning of the End", *Hindu*, April 22, 2006.

Venkateswar, Shyam and Sherchan, Sanjeev, M., "Let We Shut our Eyes off Nepal", *Indian Express*, August 11, 2006.

Vishkarma, Hiralal, *A Strategy for the Upliftment and Empowerment of Dalits*, Kathmandu, 1996.

Warren, Mark, E.(ed.), *Democracy and Trust*, Cambridge University Press, 1999.

Willett, Cyntheia (ed), *Theorizing Multiculturalism: A Guide to the Current Debate*, Blackwell, 1998.

Yechury, Sita Ram, "Till Kingdom Goes", *Hindustan Times*, April 20, 2006.

______________, "Learning from Experiences, An Analysis of Contrasting Approaches of Maoists in Nepal and India", *Economic and Political Weekly*, July 22, 2006.

Index